'OUR OLIVE'

'OUR OLIVE'

The Autobiography

of

OLIVE GIBBS

RD

ROBERT DUGDALE

OXFORD
1989

First published in 1989
by Robert Dugdale
c/o Corpus Christi College, Oxford OX1 4JF

© Olive Gibbs 1989

ISBN 0 946976 02 3

Printed in Great Britain by
Parchment (Oxford) Ltd, Printworks, Crescent Road, Cowley,
Oxford OX4 2PB

For both my families
past and present

CONTENTS

LIST OF ILLUSTRATIONS

INTRODUCTION

When I finally left the local government scene in 1986 several people who had previously been urging me to write my autobiography became more insistent. 'You must write it', they said, 'You have the time now'. They, I think without exception, were hoping for a book about the various campaigns I have been involved in. They probably had in mind a number of them: my passionate commitment to the Campaign for Nuclear Disarmament (I succeeded John Collins as National Chairman of CND in 1964, and won the Frank Cousins' Peace Award in 1986 for my contribution to peace and disarmament); the struggle against racism and, in particular, the occasion in 1967 when, with four others, I was arrested while engaged in a peaceful vigil outside a hairdresser's shop allegedly operating a colour bar, was bundled into a Black Maria and later appeared before the magistrates' bench on a charge of behaviour likely to invoke a race riot! There were also the ceaseless but frustrating attempts to remove privilege from the educational system ranging from nursery classes to the development of post-sixteen opportunitites for all our young people including the handicapped. Of special significance, in view of the current debate on inner cities, was the Battle of Jericho which was successfully fought to preserve the existing community there.

Mischievously, some of my friends would have liked an account of my turbulent years in the Oxford City Labour Party (of which I am still a member) and to recall my expulsion from the Labour Group in the late fifties for refusing to vote for a Group decision on a road through Christ Church Meadow. (I had compounded my crime by persuading five others to do the same so that the motion was lost in Council and the road never built!). I am sorry to disappoint them but one's life has to begin at birth and, as I began writing, memories of my childhood in St Thomas' district and my early formulative years came flooding back and with them the realisation that these were, perhaps, the most important years. Today's woman is but yesterday's child.

During the latter period of my time in Local Government I have twice been Lord Mayor of Oxford and had conferred on me the rare distinction of the Honorary Freedom of the City, been Chairman of Oxfordshire County Council and appointed a Deputy Lieutenant of the County, and been the recipient of the first honorary degree awarded by the Oxford Polytechnic. These years of respectability sit rather strangely on my shoulders because, for one thing, it still upsets me that even now we regard rank (birth, accent, education and dress) as more important than worth, though I too am not without sin in this respect. For another, I know at heart that the 'Mum and Granny' I now am is very little different from the 'Our Olive' I once was.

I would like to express my warm appreciation to the many people who have encouraged me to write this book and, at the same time to acknowledge the practical help I have received from Bernard Cox, Doris Ashmall, Jean Butcher, Colin Rummings, Roger Dudman, Hugo Brunner, The Very Revd E.W. Heaton (the Dean of Christ Church) and Tony Price (the former Editor of the *Oxford Times*). I am indeed grateful for their help.

OFG
August 1988

1 · SABBATH DAY CHILD

I was born on Sunday, 17 February 1918 at midday. My Aunt Sarah, my father's elder sister, delivered me on the sofa in our living room because my mother, like most working-class women of that generation, was working right up to the moment of birth and did not have time to get to bed. My twelve-year-old brother, Syd, who sang in the choir at St Thomas' Church, when given the glad tidings by his friend Walt Luckett, responded in annoyance to the news. 'Oh Blimey, a sister, I would rather have had a pair of football boots'. I have never been sure whether this demonstrated a passion for soccer or disgust at my birth. I think it was probably the former for he became an outstanding right winger for Oxford City Football Club and was even offered a contract with Aston Villa which my father would not allow him to sign on the grounds that a career in professional football was too risky.

I was the second and last child of Lazarus and Mary Ann Cox and born when my mother was thirty-nine and my father forty. My father was one of fourteen children only eight of whom survived childhood. His mother was a saint with a passion for cats as well as children. His father was a labourer, a bully and a drunk. The only person he stood in awe of was my grandmother. Once when, after a bout of drinking, he attempted to climb up the chimney while the fire was still burning, and she threatened to leave him, he resolved, so he said, to become a teatotaller. This, in fact, proved to be not total abstinence but a switch from beer to whisky.

My mother was born in Portsmouth. Her father was a Portuguese rope-maker married to an English girl, and he was crushed to death in Portsmouth Harbour when my mother was eleven years old. My poor grandmother, left with no money and with five children to feed and clothe, decided to keep the three younger children but to send her twelve-year-old boy to sea and my mother to the Nazareth Home for children in Oxford, where she was afterwards transferred to the care of the nuns at St Thomas' Convent. All her life my mother accepted with the humility of her social class and her particular brand of Christianity the necessity of this terrible sequence of events but they have never ceased to shock me and have been a driving force in my attitude to Child Care and the Welfare Services. Perhaps nothing better illustrates the incidence of child mortality and the attitude towards economic priorities of that era than the following story.

When my first son was born in 1944 he had reddish tints in his hair and I enquired, in passing, of my mother whether there was any history of red hair in our family. 'Oh yes', she replied, 'Our Charlie had red hair'. When I asked who on earth our Charlie was, since I had never heard of him before, she said, 'No dear, he was one of my younger brothers but he was drowned when he was about eighteen months old'. 'Oh Mum', I sympathised, 'what a dreadful tragedy. How on earth did it happen?'. 'Well dear', she said, 'it was my fault, I took him down to the harbour one day and forgot to put the brake on the pram. While I was playing a man called out, "Eh, Missee, is that your pram?", and I turned round and there was the pram with our Charlie in it rushing down the slipway into the sea'. 'Oh my God', I said, 'It must have haunted you ever since. Is that why you never talk about it?'. 'Not really', she said, 'I was upset about it at the time but looking back I realise that it was probably an act of God because there were far too many mouths in our family to feed', and then she added as an afterthought, 'But it was a pity about the pram. It was a good pram and we could have done with that'. I was absolutely rivetted to the spot in horror and disbelief that *my* mother, this gentle little lady who had given so much loving care to my brother and me and in fact to any children with whom she had close contact, could ever have voiced such terrible sentiments. My horror was first directed against her, but afterwards against the kind of society which induced the poor to accept such a wholly unacceptable and frightening philosophy. And people sometimes ask me why I am a socialist!

I was baptised at the Church of St Thomas the Martyr at Easter 1918 and was christened Olive Frances. Olive (Peace) was a flight of fancy on the part of my father who was in the army, as were his five brothers and two of his nephews, and was fed up with the war. I ought to be grateful I suppose that I wasn't born the following November or I might well have been called 'Poppy'. Frances was a tribute to my Uncle Frank, father's youngest brother, who was fighting in France at the time. I mention my baptism because one of my godmothers was Mother Anna Verena, the Mother Superior of St Thomas' Convent where my mother had been brought as a waif and stray some twenty-eight years before. A member of the wealthy Wills tobacco family, Mother Anna Verena was a significant influence in my early years bringing me up as a strong Anglo-Catholic, much to my father's displeasure. He had broken with St Thomas' Church when it became High Anglican (it was the second C of E church in the country to introduce the wearing of vestments) but, strong and intelligent though my father was, he was no match for this indomitable woman.

Not only was she High Church but she was a high Tory as well, and I am convinced she believed that God would expand the eye of the needle and shrink the camel in order that the rich could get into Heaven! Moreover she fervently believed as did my mother in accepting the stations to which God had called us, and that all was well with the world while the rich man remained in his castle and the poor man at his gate. Why she wanted to be my godmother, for it was she who made the approach, I do not know. It could have been for one of two reasons or for both. The first, and most obvious, is that having taken her vows as a nun she found in me the daughter she could never have. The second reason may well have been a guilty conscience, for when, in her early twenties, my mother was seen to be 'walking out' with my father who sang in the church choir they threw her out of the convent, where she was then working in the laundry, at a moment's notice. The sheer inhumanity of such an action when my mother had no family and very few friends in Oxford beggars belief. Fortunately my father's mother had a greater sense of Christian duty and took her into her already overcrowded home, eventually finding her a job in domestic service at 97 Iffley Road (which is next to the house where we now live). Her employers were a retired Indian Civil Servant and his sister, and they, bless them, gave her for several happy years a loving home life and a security which she had never before enjoyed.

We lived where I had been born, in Old Christ Church Buildings in the parish of St Thomas, between Oxford Station and Oxford Castle. Old Christ Church Buildings was built between 1846 and 1867 by Christ Church, primarily to house their college servants, although when my father took my mother there as a bride at Easter 1905 families other than those of college servants were already in occupation.

The buildings, which had a barrack-like appearance, were designed as three sides of a quadrangle and they faced on to Woodbine Place, Osney Lane and the Hamel. In the centre was a large open space for the drying of clothes but when I was young I was forbidden to set a foot in the 'drying ground' as it was an extremely unhygenic area. Some feckless families made a habit of tossing old food, bones, bottles and indescribably filthy clothes into it. On one occasion a still-born child, in a carrier bag, was discovered there but no one appeared on any charge. There was endless speculation about this gruesome find and I heard it rumoured that the child was conceived, as well as disposed of, in these unsavoury surroundings but we were a close-knit community and even if anyone knew the facts behind this discovery no one was going to 'split'.

There were eighteen one-bedroomed flats and twelve two-bedroomed flats in this two-storeyed, four-staircased building. Each landing was open but had iron railings for protection and these made excellent 'balconies' for gossip and watching the world go by, limited though the latter was.

The flats were known as the Model Buildings when they were first built and, although by present day standards they lacked many of the amenities we have now learned to expect, they were a tremendous advance on the usual standard of working-class housing of that time, and, of paramount importance, the rents were modest. In all the twenty-four years I lived there I never remember anyone being evicted.

The flats had large living rooms, bedrooms of a reasonable size and a scullery with a large copper and an indoor lavatory. The rooms had built-in cupboards and even a small store for coal off the living room. There was running water in the scullery and the living room had an oven and hob at the side of the grated fire place. Gas was beginning to be introduced, but when I was a small child the rooms were lit by oil lamps and the cooking was done in the living room on the hob or in the oven. My mother achieved the most remarkable culinary feats in these, what I would regard as impossible, conditions. On hot summer Sundays, and they seemed to be endless in those days, the cooking of the Sunday joint made the heat in the living room unbearable but most families sent the joint, surrounded by potatoes, in a baking tin to Cooper and Boffin our local baker to cook for us. It only cost two old pennies but there *were* disadvantages! The family's name used to be written on a piece of grease-proof paper and stuck firmly into the joint with a wooden skewer, but when the children went to fetch the dinner at 1 o'clock, often the grease-proof paper was burned black and the name obliterated. Then the battle royal commenced, for the children had been told in advance that if this mishap occurred they were to seize the largest non-identified joint and bring that home. Terrible fights used to break out and I have seen potatoes and often the joint itself hurled in battle. Some of the fiercest protagonists occasionally return-ed home with little or no dinner left and had their ears soundly boxed.

The lack of a bathroom did not appear to cause us any hardship. We washed in a bowl in the sink and for our weekly bath the large tin bath hanging from a hook in the scullery was put in one of the bedrooms and filled with water which had been heated on the hob. In the very cold winter months the bath was put in front of the fire in the living room and our privacy was guaranteed by a strategically placed wooden clothes horse (airer) draped with blankets.

I have often been asked if, as a child, I missed not having a garden and the plain answer to this is 'No'. This may be because you don't miss what you have never had but even today, although flowers in the house give me enormous pleasure and I am rarely without them, I can-not bear gardening because of the soil I get under my nails. What I did miss was going upstairs to bed because, in all the books I read, the children went up the stairs to their bedrooms and this did make me feel deprived.

For my father, who was born and brought up in Rewley Yard (where the Royal Oxford Hotel now stands), Old Christ Church Buildings could only compare with Buckingham Palace. When at the age of ninety-five he was incurably ill in hospital he was given the choice of staying in hospital or coming to live with me. He refused to do either and told the consultant that if he could not go back 'home' he would die. 'You can't die to order', replied the consultant, but he was mistaken: my father went on a hunger strike and died some days later. I was with him when he died and although, obviously, he was too weak to speak he opened his eyes and gave me a look of such gleeful triumph that I knew he was saying, 'You wouldn't let me go back to Old Christ Church Buildings but I beat you all in the end'. He probably believed that one of the many mansions in 'My Father's House' was modelled on the Buildings!

I was delighted when, a few years ago, the Cherwell Housing Trust negotiated an agreement with Christ Church to buy the Buildings and, while leaving the exterior unchanged, modernised the interior by introducing bathrooms and kitchens. This was not achieved without some protest from the occupants, many of whom were descended from the original families who lived there. They did not feel the need for these improvements and distrusted the whole scheme. In desperation Cherwell asked me to attend a tenants' meeting with the object of putting their fears at rest. Few compliments have given me more pleasure than Cherwell's reason for inviting me, 'You understand them, you speak the same language, they will believe you'.

2 · ST THOMAS

With the exception of about four large houses, three of which were connected in one way or another with the church, the rest of the housing in St Thomas' was working class and consisted mainly of two- and three-bedroomed terraced cottages. On the ground floor they had one 'back room' and one 'front room', which were both very small and dark, a scullery, an outside lavatory and a small garden or yard. The front room was kept immaculately cleaned and polished with bits of brass and china, 'presents from Southsea, or Weston-super-Mare', prominently displayed, together with plush-framed photographs of members of the family, mostly men in uniform. These rooms were 'hallowed places' and were never used except at Christmas and on other special occasions, particularly funerals. Because of their front rooms and gardens these tenants regarded themselves as vastly superior to those of us who lived in the Buildings. New Christ Church Buildings, built some years after the Old Buildings and now demolished, were regarded as even more inferior and we, in turn, looked down on them. No section of society was more class-conscious, and probably still is, than the working class. Most of the houses and flats were painfully overcrowded and, more often than not, housed three generations. Large numbers of children slept in the same room and four or more in the same bed was not uncommon. A family round the corner from us had a mentally handicapped child whom they kept in a shed at the bottom of the garden, not because the parents did not love her but because there was no other way, in a grossly over-crowded situation, to cope with a handicap.

Most of the desperately poor lived in yards off High Street St Thomas (now St Thomas' Street). These yards contained hovels, which had no sanitation and were built on each side of a wide gutter which appeared to have a permanent stream running down it. Occasionally ducks settled on these streams and the delighted inhabitants would catch them, wring their necks, and thus provide themselves with a Sunday meal! Little pity should be spared for these foolish birds: any self-respecting duck would have avoided these streams like the plague for more often than not they were full of garbage and sewage. Two or three of the yards contained doss houses where men who had come to seek work in Oxford existed (Billy Morris had just started up his car industry). They slept on straw and they bought their meals at Faulkner's, a shop in High Street St Thomas, which had a reputation similar to that of Harrods in that it was reputed to sell anything from a pin to a pantechnicon. A large cooked pig's head had pride of place in the shop window and the men would go in and buy two pennyworth of pig's head, one pennyworth of cooked potatoes, a slice of bread pudding, a halfpenny worth of milk in a screw of waxed paper, and other such delicacies. There were many nationalities here, a few coloured, but mostly Irish and Italian. There were also one or two isolated prostitutes, but it wasn't until I was much older that I realised what they were, for my mother always euphemistically referred to them as 'girls who were no better than they should be'. It was, in many ways, the Soho of Oxford and there were always at least two policemen together at any one time on the beat.

In the north-west corner of the parish a few yards from the Railway Station was the church, founded sometime in the twelfth century in honour of Thomas à Becket, 'the turbulent priest'. My parents were married there and I was baptised, confirmed and married there. It was, however, not the only religious influence, for the Salvation Army Citadel was a few minutes walk away, in Castle Street, and in High Street St Thomas was the Chapel. This was a tin-roofed building presided over by a Miss Hughes, who lived somewhere in North Oxford. Her interest for me is that, many years later, I discovered that before my election to the City Council, in 1953, she was the only woman ever to have represented the West Ward on the Council. She won a seat in 1908. I know so little about the Chapel because, again, the distinction between attending Church and going to Chapel was a social one and we, the Lord's preferred, were never allowed near it. I don't think it had any minister attached to it but was serviced by lay preachers. What I do know was that Miss Hughes ministered, in a very practical way, to the poor, for she was as much concerned with nourishing their bodies as she was with saving their souls. They all loved her and she is remembered to this day. I am proud to have followed her.

On the other side of Osney Lane was St Thomas' Church School where most of the children of the parish were educated from nursery school age until they reached compulsory school leaving age which was then fourteen years. It was built on a site donated by Christ Church in 1904 and 1905, and, except for the Head's room at one end of the school, was all at ground floor level, with a tarmac surround which also served as a playground. In the front it had some fine iron railings but I remember these railings with pain for I once put my head through them not realising that my ears, small though they were, would prevent me from freeing myself. I was painfully stuck there for what seemed eternity . My mother and the neighbours rubbed soap behind my ears, covering my hair with grease and alternately pulling my legs and pushing my head, or, even worse, doing both simultaneously. It was agonising and my admiration and affection for the Fire Service dates from that day, some sixty years ago, when they arrived and cut me free.

Immediately opposite us was the 'rec', our recreation ground owned by the City Council and looked after somewhat inadequately by a 'keeper' who had several other recreation grounds under his control. It boasted a shelter, two sets of swings, and a maypole. The maypole was as different from the current image of maypoles, with brightly coloured plaited ribbons, as it is possible to imagine. It was a stout wooden pole to which were attached at the top heavy chains with wooden handles dangling from them about 4ft from the ground. It was rarely used for the purpose for which it was intended and a favourite sport was to lift a chain as high as possible and then send it crashing round. Often children were badly cut and bruised but it was only when one boy was seriously injured and had to be taken to hospital that it was dismantled. Goal posts were not in evidence in my day, although I believe they appeared later, and when team games were played a pile of coats marked the goal. But the main enjoyment of the 'rec' for us was the making of sack-cloth tents and fishing for stickle-backs in the Castle Stream which flowed through the east side. We impaled the sacks on the iron railings and then secured them to the ground with pieces of sharpened wood and large flat stones. Once when we were short of sacks I crept home and removed the blankets from my bed. When I returned home with filthy torn blankets my mother was angrier than I have ever seen her and threatened to send me to a home. This was not an uncommon threat to children but it had never been made to me before and I was terrified. Just outside these tents we lit fires and cooked potatoes and other food we had stolen. Why no one was burned to death I cannot imagine but perhaps the devil looked after his own! Our fishing expeditions were just as dangerous: we climbed the spiked railings and with a home-made fishing net and a jam jar for our catches we flirted with death when the river was high. Next to the 'rec' were stables and a riding school. I don't know who owned these but my mother was fond of telling me that the 'dear prince' (The Prince of Wales, later Edward VIII) often came there to ride when he was an undergraduate. It was through this riding school that I first discovered my disastrous tendency to faint (a disposition which has bedevilled me all my life) for, on joining a crowd which had gathered outside the school, I saw a horse impaled on the railings; I felt a funny buzzing in my head and woke up to find myself on our sofa at home.

There were four pubs in St Thomas: the Marlborough Arms, the Turk's Head and the Chequers in High Street and in Hollybush Row was the Albion. At our end of Osney Lane was Morrell's Brewery which stretched behind the Hamel into High Street St Thomas. It had a very tall chimney which we were always afraid would fall on us. Its large wooden gates, through which the beer drays went, provided excellent material for chalking up goal posts and wickets for the endless games of football and cricket we played in the streets. I always joined in these games which infuriated my grandfather. One day he watched me from one of the Buildings' balconies until his fury exploded and he sought out my father and said, 'Look at her, look at her running the streets with those boys. Mark my words, my son, she'll come to no good.' When the freedom of the City of Oxford was conferred on me in 1982, uppermost in my mind was my grandfather's prophecy and I am sure he would have been horrified and astounded that the City of Oxford, of which he was an hereditary freeman, had become so degenerate as to accord this honour to me.

We so rarely saw a car in the streets that if one appeared it was an object of great interest. My grandfather regarded cars as an 'invention of the devil' and he and a mate sometimes stood on the pavement near the Railway Station and as one of these 'infernal machines' approached they would put their hands in their pockets and throw a handful of broken glass and nails in its path. Horse-drawn carts brought our bread, our milk, our vegetables and our coal. Once a week we had a visit from 'Banana Annie'. Ada Lappage, a staunch supporter of the Salvation Army, was a short, fat lady of indeterminate age, with a black beard which fascinated us. She wore a man's cloth cap, men's boots and voluminous black calico skirts. She walked at a permanent angle of almost ninety degrees, pushing her barrow and shouting 'Ripe bananas, ripe bananas, six a penny, ripe bananas'. Ripe they certainly were, of a squishy black variety, but we loved them.

Describing the physical conditions existing in St Thomas' during my childhood is much less difficult than attempting to recapture the life and spirit of that remarkable community. We were all poor, even by the standards of that period, and I remember my father's bitter comment that 'when Britain was the richest industrial country in the world he and his brothers were looking in dustbins for food', but there were differing degrees of poverty among us and we provided our own kind of welfare system. In light of man's innate selfishness 'loving thy neighbour as thyself' is an impossible conception but we came as near to it in St Thomas' as I have seen it anywhere else in my life. Few of us who lived in this, or similar, communities will ever condone the crass stupidity of the planners, both pre-war and post-war, who razed to the ground most of the housing in the inner City areas, replaced it with offices and industrial buildings and sent the displaced families to live on various housing estates on the fringes of the City where they felt isolated and alienated. Millions of pounds were then spent on creating community associations and centres, worthy objectives in themselves, but incapable of producing the same kind of communities which they, the planners, had wantonly destroyed.

It is a sad reflection on our times, and indicative of the loneliness and isolation of so many people, that we see, almost daily in our newspapers, accounts of persons dying or dead, without anyone being aware of the fact for several days. This could never have happened in St Thomas'. We were at pains, for there appeared to be an inborn delicacy among us, not to make unwarranted intrusions on individual privacy but we always knew what was going on and we shared each other's happiness and sorrows. We shared our food when it was needed and, if the necessity arose, we shared our homes. Living above our flat was a family called Mold, a father and three sons. The youngest, Charlie, was about my age and the other two were several years older. The mother had died when Charlie was a baby and Mr Mold, who worked on the railway, kept his family together with the assistance of neighbours. On at least two occasions I remember being awakened in the early hours of the morning by a timid tapping on our front door, which gradually increased to a frenzied fortissimo. My mother was out of bed like a flash. 'Quick, Olive', she said, 'put the kettle on. It's young Charlie'. When she opened the door it was indeed young Charlie who, with tears pouring down his face, fell into her arms saying, 'Mrs Cox, can you come quick. Me Dad's been took bad'. With instructions to me to make Charlie a cup of cocoa she flew upstairs and having made 'Dad' comfortable she rushed back in to us, put a coat over her nightdress and ran all the way to Gloucester Green to fetch an ambulance. While the ambulance men were bringing Mr Mold down on a stretcher she told me to make a bed for Charlie on our sofa and then went off to the Radcliffe Infirmary in the ambulance and waited at the hospital until she was sure that Mr Mold was being attended to before she returned home. It was taken for granted that Charlie would then stay with us, as a non-paying guest, until his father came home. I think Mr Mold had an ulcer which is not altogether surprising in view of the fact that he did a full time job on the railway as well as looking after his family and it was something of a hand to mouth existence. I think Charlie viewed his father's return with mixed feelings for, although he quite obviously adored his Dad, he did enjoy my mother's cooking which I found not difficult to understand after he had recounted one of his dreams to me. 'I had a lovely dream last night, Olive. I dreamt the Gas Works exploded and we was all blown up'. 'I don't think that was a very nice dream, Charlie', I replied rather prissily, 'it sounds more like a nightmare to me'. 'Well', he said, 'when I was blowed up I landed in Faulkner's window and I was just about to grab a slice of the pig's head when I woke up. I was ever so disappointed'.

As children we followed very closely our parents' pattern of behaviour and, with very few exceptions, shared most of our things, meagre though they were. If one of us, with our weekly penny, bought six of Annie's ripe bananas we kept one for ourselves and gave one each to five of our friends knowing we would be repaid by an appropriate share in their purchases of gob-stoppers, licorice braids, sherbet dabs, mint humbugs, and pop-corn. I once broke this ethical code in a disgustingly mean and shabby way, the memory of which can still flood me with shame. This disgraceful incident happened outside Butt's general shop at the corner of Woodbine Place and the High

Street. I rounded the corner and bumped into one of my closest friends Cyril Dean. He was about a year younger than me, a good looking boy with dark curly hair and the eldest of a family of six. His father, who worked in the building industry, was often out of work in bad weather, and Cyril's Mum took in washing from the big houses and the shops to help out the family finances. On this particular day he was carrying a large wicker laundry basket, full of washing, and he could scarcely see over the top. As we chatted he suddenly exclaimed, 'Coo, look, there's sixpence on the pavement'. As quick as lightning, and before he could put down his basket, I snatched the sixpence and made off with it. What is even worse is that my conscience pricked me afterwards and I bought him a ½d Sherbet dab. I often think this wretched betrayal is second only to Judas Iscariot's, for Cyril was my devoted friend and I knew his family was much poorer than mine. When I read, during the war, that he went down with HMS *Hood* and was drowned in a sea of burning oil I was filled with unbearable remorse, as well as sorrow. Occasionally my friends tell me I shall get into Heaven not through any virtue on my part but because St Peter will get fed up with arguing with me at the Gate. Little do they know that I am guilty of one sin I can never argue my way through. The dreadful thing is that if anyone is going to argue my case with St Peter it will be Cyril for he was that sort of kid.

With the exception of the High Street yards there was very little unemployment in St Thomas'. The men for the most part were employed in unskilled jobs in the local, mainly service, industries. In addition to the college servants (and in 1914 the University was the biggest single employer in Oxford), they worked on the railway, in the gas works, at the brewery, as building labourers, in shops and for the Oxford City Corporation. Quite a number worked at the Oxford University Press in Walton Street and many at Cooper's Marmalade Factory in Park End Street. Few of the women with children worked outside the home, except those who were widowed or whose husbands were ill, and they took in washing or cleaned in shops and offices. The poverty was caused by large families and low wages. Many years later, in 1974, when as Lord Mayor I was dining on High Table at one of the Oxford colleges, a crusty old don droned on and on about the disaster caused to Oxford by 'that fellah Morris' building his wretched car factory here. 'Do you know', he demanded of those of us who were still awake, 'before that fellah came here we based our college servants' wages on those of agricultural workers?'. A bright pretty young woman sitting opposite me raised her bored head and said loudly, 'That figures, I suppose. Same job – looking after pigs'. I could have hugged her.

In the light of the comparatively high wages paid at the Cowley factory it was surprising that so few of the men in the older areas of the City were tempted to go and work there and, in the early days, Billy

Morris recruited most of his labour force from the distressed areas in the North of England and from the closing pits in the Welsh Valleys. I think caution played a large part in this and men were afraid to give up steady employment for what might prove to be a disastrous new venture.

I personally only knew one man in St Thomas' who gave up his job on the railway and went to work at Cowley. He was the father of one of my friends, Joan Gibson. Joan was the envy of all the girls at St Thomas' School. She had dazzling satin dresses, tied with shiny ribbon bows, and patent leather shoes with straps. These were in sharp contrast to our dull serviceable dresses and stout laced shoes. Moreover there was always keen competition to secure an invitation to tea at the Gibsons because there were always unheard of treats like tomato, cucumber and egg sandwiches, jam doughnuts coated with coconut and, on occasions, the never-before-tasted tinned pink salmon. It made a luxurious change from the inevitable salmon and shrimp paste sandwiches which were the standard fare for tea in most of our homes. My father in later years loved recounting to my sons the occasion on which I asked him whether the King and Queen were as rich as the Gibsons!

Tea at the Gibsons was not the only highlight of our social life, for as well as birthdays and Christmas there always seemed to be something to look forward to. In the summer we took our tea down the 'rec' and, although this only meant transferring the bread and jam and paste sandwiches from home to the outdoors, there was a special flavour to it and we could always go 'butterfly chasing' between courses. In the spring we went bluebelling and primrosing in Hen Wood; the journey to which along Botley Road, Ferry Hinksey Lane, and Willow Walk provided many exciting adventures. We walked everywhere as none of us had bicycles but occasionally we would 'club together' and hire a bike from a shop in Church Street, St Ebbes, for 2d an hour. Heaven knows what state the bikes were in when we returned them because we used to pedal at break-neck speed round all the streets in St Thomas', more often than not on the pavements, to the danger and fury of our parents.

There were also Sunday School treats and Sunday School outings for which our mothers paid small weekly sums in advance. My brother Syd, returning from one of these treats, was asked by my mother, anxious to find out whether she was getting value for her money, what he had had to eat.

'One cherry', said Syd.

'One cherry', exclaimed my mother in astonishment, 'wasn't there anything else to eat?'. And when she was told tearfully that there were cakes, sandwiches and jellies, in addition to the cherries, she demanded furiously why he had only had one cherry.

'Because I didn't know what to do with the stone, Mum', he sobbed.

I was made of sterner stuff and well remember the occasion when we went on a Sunday School outing, by charabanc, to Weston-super-Mare. When we got there I decided to spend one of my pennies on a donkey ride. All went well until the donkey was stung by a wasp and raced at a speed which would have done credit to a Derby winner, to the sea. We seemed to cover miles and miles of mud flats, now described in holiday brochures as Weston's golden sands, until we reached the water. During this terrifying race I managed to cling on, but only to the underbelly of the donkey, and in the process lost my tea-ticket. I don't think I expected sympathy for this hair-raising experience for I was already cynical about adults' reactions to children's misfortunes, and I guessed they would suspect me of deliberately turning the donkey's nose in the direction of the wasp, but I did expect to get my tea as my Mum had already paid for it, so I was absolutely furious when the organisers told me I couldn't have it as I hadn't got a ticket. I argued, I shouted, I stamped, but it was only when I threatened to force my way into the hall and seize what was on the trestle tables that they, reluctantly, let me in.

When summer was almost over we had 'St Giles' Fair' to look forward to. Two extra days at the beginning of September were always officially added to our five weeks school summer holidays for this great event. For weeks in advance we used to save for 'The Fair'. There was never anything to spare out of our 'weekly penny' but there were always other ways of making money. We did odd jobs, we ran errands; we collected jam jars and rabbit skins and took them to Warburtons, the rag and bone merchants in St Ebbes. I wasn't much good with the rabbit skins because I always fainted when I picked one up but the other kids were very good and took mine for me. We also paid unusual 'courtesy calls' on our relations; not altogether unexpected as far as they were concerned, for they always had a few coppers saved in a jar on the mantelpiece to give us for the Fair. Most of us kept our savings in small tin money boxes which could be locked and the keys given to our parents for safe keeping. Occasionally when a financial disaster arose, like losing our weekly penny down the drain or over-indulging ourselves with ripe bananas or sherbet dabs, the urge to recoup our losses was overwhelming, and unknown to our parents we got a table knife and inserted the blade into the slot of the money box. This slot was only just big enough to take a penny but by careful manipulation and much shaking we could usually manage to slide a few halfpennies down the blade. In spite of these 'bank raids', by the time the great day dawned we had amassed a fortune – anything from one shilling to half-a-crown and with infinite care we stretched it over the two days. There was plenty to spend it on: penny rides on the round-abouts, usually prancing horses; shying at coco-nuts; jolting ourselves almost sick on the cake-walk; licking great lumps of brown and white mint humbug, plaited before our very eyes by rather dirty hands, all this to the accompaniment of loud music from the splendid, brightly-coloured organs driven by steam engines, and with gold coloured military figures made in metal on the front, which realistically beat drums or raised their arms in salute. There were also Wild West Shows with a platform outside on which 'Cowboys' would lassoo one another and girls, highly painted and scantily dressed, would prance up and down. Outside the boxing booths male members of the public were stridently invited in to see if they could beat 'The Champ' but I wouldn't go anywhere near these in case I saw someone with a bloodied nose.

We did not bother to waste our money on seeing 'The Fat Lady', 'The Bearded Lady' or 'the Fortune Teller' for fat ladies were not uncommon in St Thomas' and we could view Banana Annie's beard for free once a week. Moreover, as far as the Fortune Teller was concerned, our parents were only too anxious to warn us at frequent intervals of the dire fate awaiting us if we continued to carry on in the way we did.

Not only did we enjoy the Fair itself, but few of us ever missed the excitement of the Fair 'drawing in'. In those days, no fair stall or round-about was allowed in St Giles until 6 am on the first day of the Fair and we used to get up at 4 am, knocking up the lay-abeds, and watched the caravans, steam-driven engines and 'amusements' slowly move in to the centre of Oxford from the surrounding areas. Unlike today, when sites are allocated in advance, the first in acquired the prime sites, and I remember that to be the 'first' was an honour much coveted by the fair-ground people. Many years later, I and other city councillors, mainly those who were also born and bred in Oxford, fiercely resisted attempts, by a group of city councillors who had not had our colourful childhood experiences, to remove on traffic grounds, the Fair from St Giles to the outskirts of the City. We were successful, but I believe the rot has set in because for the past two years Oxford children have not been given their official two days' holiday for the Fair.

On the Wednesday morning after the Fair we were plunged into a Slough of Despond. The summer was over, the Fair was gone and we were back at school, sitting in serried rows, chanting tables parrot fashion, and having our knuckles rapped with a ruler if we spoke out of turn or uttered a double negative. I always felt very aggrieved about the latter, because I felt that the use of the double negative in 'Please Miss, I ain't got no ink', added urgency to my desperate situation.

The next major event on our social calendar was Bonfire Night on November 5th. For weeks beforehand we collected all kinds of bonfire material: old chairs, mattresses, cardboard boxes, in fact anything that was inflammable. There was sometimes an added bonus in this for not only were we accumulating material for the 'biggest bonfire you have ever seen', but we were occasionally given a few coppers for carting it away. This money we used for buying 'sparklers' and a few fireworks

– our chief delights being 'Catherine Wheels' and 'Jumping Jacks'. We were not impressed by rockets which at 4d each were very expensive and were over all too quickly with a single bang or whimper.

Originally we stored all our accumulated rubbish in the covered passage-way leading to the drying ground for it was in the drying ground that those of us who lived in the Buildings and were without gardens held our communal remembrance of Guy Fawkes' attempt to blow up Parliament. After a few years, partly because our mothers couldn't get through the passage-way to hang out their washing but more importantly because the fire became so large it was a danger to the surrounding flats, we transferred it to the 'rec'. This posed difficulties for when the 'rec' keeper was in a black mood he threatened to call the local bobby unless we removed 'all this bloody junk' from his shelter; and we had hurriedly to disperse it to allotment sheds, sculleries and wash-houses and some back to the drying ground passage. Our parents were extraordinarily understanding about this, because, I think, they knew how much this meant to us, and also because it kept us out of worse mischief. Our Guy was not only the most splendid I have ever seen but it was also a magnificent example of co-operative effort. It was taken for granted that we would have one St Thomas' Guy and not waste our time on individual effigies. For its body we filled a large coal sack with straw, rags and paper, and for its arms and legs we similarly filled old trouser legs. Its head was any old pillow-case or cushion cover, torn to size, and stuffed. We then dressed it in clothes which were left over, or purloined, from jumble sales. Our only expense was a hideous mask we bought from the Penny Bazaar in St Ebbes Street. When this work of art was finished, we mounted it on a carriage made by attaching a board to a set of old pram wheels, and for a couple of weeks before the Night we trundled it round the streets, sometimes as far as the station, begging a 'penny for the Guy' with heart-warming financial success. The 'Grads' (undergraduates) were particularly generous and we made lots of money to buy fireworks with. It was typical of the code which existed between us, call it honour among thieves if you like, that we could always trust whoever went out with the Guy to bring the money back. We got attached to our 'creation' over the weeks and some of us had tears in our eyes when it was eventually tossed on to the Bonfire at the height of the blaze but we would never admit to such a stupid weakness and blamed it on the smoke. But at the beginning of September 'Bonfire Night' was a long way off, so for those of us who hadn't birthdays in September or October, dreary days stretched endlessly ahead and we had to create our own excitements. They were classified by our parents as both wicked and dangerous and looking back I think they were.

To our God-fearing parents our games of cowboys and Indians in the churchyard were nothing short of sacrilege, for the cowboys sat astride the tombstones pretending they were horses while the Indians

crouched down on the graves themselves, disturbing the soil and van-
dalising the flowers. When we grew tired of this, or were chased out of
the churchyard by the godly, we made our way to the junction of
Becket Street and Osney Lane where there was an iron bridge across
the railway line, known locally as The Black Bridge. I shudder to think
of it now but we would dare one another to perform the 'tight-rope
act'. This meant walking on the narrow parapets of the bridge from
one end of it to the other with nothing to hang on to, or to steady
ourselves with. The greatest dare of all was to do it when a train was
just puffing towards us from Oxford Station so that we would be
enveloped in clouds of steam. That no child ever fell was a miracle and
one we did not deserve so soon after our godless behaviour in the
churchyard.

A much less dangerous game but one which irritated our parents
almost beyond endurance was tying door knobs together. We would
steal a number of washing lines from the drying ground and proceed to
tie them firmly to the door knobs of two adjacent houses; in the
Buildings we could improve on this by linking *three* doors together! We
then did a sharp rat-a-tat-tat on the doors and scampered off staying
just close enough to hear the muttered oaths of people trying to open
their doors. The harder each of them pulled, the more firmly he or she
shut his neighbours' door. Eventually, of course, either the knot
loosened, or the rope broke, and they could free themselves, emerging
purple in the face from both their exertions and their fury. We were
too far away by then to witness their shaking fists and their threats to
kill us if they ever found out which of us had done it. These threats
were reiterated when our mums went to hang the washing out and
found their lines had gone.

There were attractions for us, too, outside the parish. Those of us who
could afford it went to the pictures on Saturday afternoons. The old
George Street cinema, which stood on the site of the present cinema,
gave matinée performances which cost us four old pennies for a three-
hour programme. These programmes were not arranged specifically
for children nor was the audience restricted to children, for adults
could get in by paying nine-pence. The standard fare was one major
film, one minor film, and an extract from a serial which ran for about
three weeks. A typical afternoon's delight would be a cowboy and Indian film, with Tom Mix or Jackie Coogan in it, a shorter film about a
faithful and resourceful dog called 'Rin Tin Tin' and a breathtaking
serial called 'Pearl White and the Clutching Hand'. Pearl White – so
aptly named as she was a beautiful innocent young virgin — was
always getting into the hands of a greasy-haired villain. The extract
always finished with poor Pearl in a perilous position from which it
would appear impossible for her to extricate herself and ended with the
caption, 'Did she fall, or was she pushed? Come and find out next

week'. I still remember the frustration I felt when chicken-pox prevented me from returning one particular Saturday and my friends' report on Pearl's remarkable escape from the perilous plight she was in was so inadequate.

These were the days of silent films, but the whole programme was shown to the accompaniment of a piano recital. At the beginning of each show a platform, with a piano and with a lady sitting on a piano stool, would be levered up through a trap door immediately in front of the screen. What a heroic performance, unmatched by anything we saw on film, this lady gave. For a short while, before the first film began, she gave us renderings of all the current popular songs, but once the film started she matched her music to the action on the screen; fortissimo as the cowboys and Indians thundered across the Plains, and pianissimo as the hero put his arm round the heroine's waist. As Rin Tin Tin lay wounded and dying the music was so sad it brought tears to our eyes. This remarkably talented lady and her piano were always positioned side-ways from the audience but whether this was so we could see her, or whether she dared not turn her back to us I don't know. We did not sit quietly through the show but shouted loudly in support of our heroes and booed when the villain appeared. On the rare occasions when we got bored we started fights between ourselves. When we got too noisy there were shouts from the adults for us to be removed but this sanction was only imposed by management when we were guilty of throwing missiles, and then we were summarily ejected. But this rarely happened, for when we were thrown out we dared not go home on our own and face our parents. We had to wait outside the cinema, often in the cold, until our mates came out.

Of far more benefit to our minds and bodies were the recreational facilities of the Balliol Boys' Club in St Ebbes. Alas as the name implied it was restricted to boys only, but it catered in a way no other organisation did for the recreational and leisure needs of working-class boys and youths living in St Thomas' and St Ebbes. There was a similar club, the Worcester Boys' Club, in St Clements which served the St Clements and East Oxford areas. Financed by the colleges and run, except for the assistance of paid club leaders, voluntarily by undergraduates, the boys were taught football, swimming, table-tennis and billiards. During the summer vacation they were able to go for a week's camping holiday near the sea or the mountains. The present Lord Mayor's Sergeant, Mr Sid Rowland, who belonged to the Worcester Boys' Club, pays warm tribute to the social work of these clubs. 'They provided marvellous opportunities for us boys and a good many of us would never have had a holiday except for them'.

There were no such opportunities for the girls. We could join the Brownies and the Girl Guides but few of us did because the uniforms were expensive and the attitude towards us condescending. I joined, but no sooner had my mother finished paying for the uniform than I was thrown out for being thoroughly unsuitable material. This I think was entirely justified for, during a concert in Wesley Hall, I and two others, crept beneath the stage and, during the finale when Brown Owl, Tawny Owl, and a whole gaggle of owls were singing in a nasal Oxford accent, 'We ah heah together agen, we ah heah, we ah heah, we ah heah together agen we ah heah, we ah heah, and who knows when we'll be altogether agen singing altogether agen we ah heah', we removed the props supporting the stage and they all sank 'below stairs' in an undignified heap!

Two or three times a year when all other pleasures had palled we would decide to wage war on the Friars, that part of St Ebbes which was closest to us across the 'rec'. The raid would begin with a hail of small stones lobbed from the waste ground and allotments which adjoined the 'rec', where the Oxford College of Further Education now stands, and when the enemy had been tempted out the real battle began. This was not unarmed combat, although now and again the boys would resort to fisticuffs and the girls to hair pulling, but we used any weapons we could lay our hands on – sticks, stones and half bricks. It did not last long because, with much whistle-blowing, the local bobbies would arrive, box our ears and send us home. Two or three weeks later there would be a retaliatory raid from the Friars but honour having been appeased things would go quiet for a while although a state of cold war always existed between us. I never heard of anyone being seriously injured although some of us carry our battle scars to this day – mine a 'dimple' on one cheek only, from an encounter with a youthful fist.

We always thought of the Friars kids as untouchables – a vastly inferior social class from ourselves – and I was amazed to discover, years later, that they regarded us in exactly the same way. In fact we were known to all the adjoining areas as the 'Tomrags' a highly contemptuous term.

I am often asked whether my childhood was a happy one and I invariably reply that it was but that is not the whole truth. From what I have already written it is obvious that my early life in St Thomas' itself was rich in colourful experiences, laughter and friendship, and I would not have missed any of it, but my home life was rather different. Edmund, my husband, who was brought up in a professional progressive family, is aghast at what he sees as the brutality of my own upbringing, but what he fails to understand is that the working class of that period valued highly the Victorian ideas of never sparing the rod to spoil the child, and of allowing the male complete and absolute domination of his family, practices which were typical of family life in St Thomas'. In many ways, because of my father's character, I was subjected to more physical and psychological violence than most of my friends, but equally he set me standards and implanted in me principles which other children did not have, and which have stood me in good stead all my life. I was afraid of him until he died but I gave up hating him many years ago and I have a lot to be grateful to him for. His bitterness and frustration, coupled with his desire for a better life for me, are perhaps best illustrated in the following, for me, very moving experience.

About twenty years ago, when he was in his eighties, he was reading a report in the *Oxford Times* about the leading part I had played in the scheme to rehabilitate Jericho, and he looked up and said, 'I often used to wonder, our Olive, why I was born: always hungry as a kid, going to work at eleven years old and not finishing until I was sixty-five, too old and too tired to enjoy anything. Not much point to that sort of life but now I keep reading in the paper about the things you do as a councillor and I realise I was born to bring you up, and give you an education of sorts, so that you could work for the likes of us'.

In fairness to my father, and in an attempt to look objectively at those days which stretched from early childhood right through to my twenties, I believe, in retrospect, that he loved me dearly and was anxious to bring me up in what he considered to be the right way. Moreover, from other people's recollections, I am persuaded that I was not the easiest of children to discipline, for I had inherited his aggressive tendencies and his stubbornness. This is borne out by the fact that my brother, who like my mother had a loving docile nature, incurred my father's wrath much less often than I did, although he too was not immune from my father's attempts to dictate to him, even after his marriage.

It was the nature of my various punishments that I so bitterly resented, and I still do. There were days when I knew in advance that whatever answer I gave to one of my father's questions I should be punished, and punished severely, because he was in 'that sort of mood'. If in reply to a simple question like 'Are you wearing a vest, Olive?' I said 'No' he would accuse me of immodesty. If, on the other hand, I had replied 'Yes' I would have been found guilty of mollycoddling myself, and in both cases swift retribution would follow. Corporal punishment would sometimes be inflicted by a cane which he kept in the cupboard but more often by hand because this enabled him to act more quickly if he was in one of his ungovernable rages. He would rain blows on my head and my face until I said I was sorry. Apologies were always difficult to extract from me and when one was not immediately forthcoming the worst of all punishments would follow. He would lock me in the clothes cupboard in the bedroom, and I can remember to this day the panic and fear which engulfed me as the key turned in the lock. The darkness was terrible and the clothes hanging round me seemed to be suffocating me. I used to beat on the door with my fists and it didn't take long for me to scream 'sorry' but he would leave me there for a bit to 'teach me a lesson'. Once, when I was sent to bed for getting my shoes wet, I was kneeling by the bed saying my prayers, and he stormed into the bedroom, yanked me to my feet and said I was too wicked to pray! My mother sometimes tried to intervene but then his wrath was turned on her.

In recent debates on the abolition of corporal punishment I have been horrified when some members of the Education Committee have got to their feet and said, proudly, 'Six of the best never did me any harm'. Well, except for inspiring in me a strongly held belief that violence, whether it is corporal punishment, capital punishment or war, is evil, they did me a great deal of harm. When in 1954, after years of almost unbearable tensions, I was in hospital with a nervous breakdown, my psychiatrist had no difficulty in attributing it to these early experiences, and moreover assured me that I could never be completely cured, and free from tensions, until I broke entirely from my father. This I could never do as he always thought he had been a good father to me and, according to his lights, he was. Even today there are occasions when I think, 'Oh, my God, how on earth am I going to explain this to Dad?' and a wave of relief sweeps over me as I realise I have no need to!

He also regarded 'vanity' as one of the deadliest of sins and I grew up believing myself to be extremely plain (which, from photographs, I was obviously not) and with very few compensating virtues. I was rarely praised and frequently compared unfavourably with my brother or some of my cousins, but instead of producing the kind of modesty he had hoped for this treatment gave me basic feelings of insecurity from which I still suffer and which I cover with an outward show of belligerence.

By working-class standards of that day we lived very comfortably, for, from an economic viewpoint, we were virtually a one child family: by the time I was two my brother, who left school at fourteen, was employed at the *Oxford Times* as an office boy and two years later he became a cub reporter. My father, having left school to work at the Queen's College, where he opened doors for the 'young gentlemen' to pass through and was not infrequently knocked down in the process, was afterwards apprenticed to a firm of printers, George Bryant, which was in a yard off Cornmarket Street where the Co-op now stands. Having served his apprenticeship, he was a printer pressman journeyman which, I think, qualified him as a master printer. He was a good workman, intelligent and conscientious, and worked for the same firm for the rest of his life even when it was acquired by the Alden Press.

He worked for thirty shillings a week which never seemed to vary, for inflation appears to be a comparatively recent phenomenon. He paid a sum of three shillings and two-pence a week for our flat, three shillings for the rent and two-pence for the rates, and this money was collected weekly by one of Christ Church's rent collectors. Our outgoings were small, and carefully and intelligently budgetted. We paid into three small weekly insurances; the first two paid out lump sums after a set period of years and this money was not only useful, but essential, for meeting what were to us large capital outlays, like replacing furniture and other necessities. The third was paid out only on death and, among other things, would cover any funeral expenses. The latter was a *must* in any respectable St Thomas' family, for the possibility of a pauper's grave was too terrible to contemplate. I have never fully understood this particular fear and cannot make up my mind whether it was assumed that entrance to Heaven would take longer from a pauper's grave or whether a life-time's failure should not be evident after death.

Our health needs were met by the Cutler Boulter Penny-a-Week Dispensary in Gloucester Green. The penny covered each individual for all medical care, doctors and prescriptions. Whether there was a reduction for family membership I do not know, but my father regarded it as money well spent as indeed it was. So much so that, when the National Insurance Act (embodying the main proposals of the Beveridge Report) was introduced in 1947, from the personal health angle we could see little difference from what we had already enjoyed, for what a splendid band of doctors it was who worked for the dispensary. Each winter I suffered from serious and very distressing bouts of bronchitis, and at the onslaught of one of these attacks my mother would rush to the dispensary with a note. Within a very short time, as I lay in bed with a very high fever, I would hear the clop clop of horses' hooves and know that my dearly-loved Dr Thompson, the doctor allocated to minister to the needs of our family, had arrived in his pony and trap. He was such a kindly, caring man that the minute he came through the door every patient felt comforted. What happened to those poor unfortunates who wouldn't, or couldn't, pay the penny a week I don't know. The illness I most dreaded contracting was scarlet fever for, in those days, immediately it was diagnosed one was rushed off to the Isolation Hospital on the Abingdon Road and incarcerated there for a full eight weeks. Moreover any house where this disease had been notified had a red sign painted on the door and was avoided like the plague.

We were always well fed. My father used to say that money spent on food was never wasted. For breakfast we had an egg or bacon and on Sundays, luxury of luxuries, we had both. Our main meal, dinner, was at mid-day, as it was for the vast majority of families in this country, and my father like other men came home for it. We always had meat in some form or another: roast on Sundays and minced on Mondays which was washing day for all women in St Thomas rain or shine. I can still smell that damp smell of drying clothes all over the house on a wet Monday! We had steak and kidney puddings, toad in the hole, liver and onions, rabbit stew, mutton stew and, on high days and holidays, a chicken. My father was in advance of his times in believing in a balanced diet, and we always had a green vegetable as well as potatoes and, on his instructions, my mother rarely resorted to a frying pan. We had puddings every day: rice, stewed fruit, steamed puddings and all, except the rice, with Pearce Duff custard. On Sundays we had tinned peaches, pears, or pineapple, with custard or cream.

Tea, which we had between 5.30 and 6 pm, was bread with jam or paste, and biscuits and home-made cake. For my father, as in other working-class homes, there was, in addition, always something more substantial: kippers, bloaters, smoked haddock or a $\frac{1}{4}$lb. of ham. We, too, enjoyed these 'treats' at weekends. In the summer, because of my father's conviction that extra vitamin C should be added to our diet, we had lots of lettuce, tomatoes, celery and water cress. In the winter, bread was often replaced by toast and crumpets, cooked on a long fork which was always kept by the side of the grated fire. At bedtime I had a cup of cocoa and a biscuit, but in warmer weather a glass of milk replaced the hated cocoa. Supper for my parents was at 10 pm: bread and cheese, pickles and a glass of beer, the latter fetched in a jug by my mother from the Marlborough Arms. We never used anything but butter and fresh milk, and although I did not miss the margarine of my friends' homes I was bitterly envious of their tinned condensed milk, a lovely and very sweet substitute for milk and sugar which graced most of their tables, and which plunged me into a seventh heaven of delight when they gave me a spoonful. When visitors called at unexpected times, they were regaled with biscuits, a piece of cake and a cup of tea or Camp Coffee. Fruit in our house was plentiful which was unusual in the area, and my brother once told me that someone had said 'The Coxes must be ever so rich 'cos' they've got grapes on their sideboard even when nobody's ill'. Since Syd, as far as the lighter side of life was concerned, had a tendency never to spoil a good story with the truth I can't vouch for the accuracy of this statement!

My father had an obsession about hygiene. He would never eat or drink outside the home for fear the eating utensils weren't properly washed. Few if any families in St Thomas' ever ate out, but once week-ly, at least, usually on pay day, they fetched their own 'take-aways': fish and chips in newspaper from Denton's in Castle Street or Carlo's or Delnevo's in St Ebbes, and faggots and peas in one's own basin from Trip Whittam's (he also sold tripe) in Castle Street. The cost was 2d for a generous portion of cod fried in batter and a penny extra for the chips. Two large, deliciously smelling meat faggots, with a basinful of thick savoury gravy and peas, were 4d. I can smell those delicious mouth watering smells to this day but I was forbidden not only to buy any but even to accept a 'taste' from my friends. This ban also applied to the toffee apples made by a family living in one of the yards in St Thomas' but this I can understand more readily for it was quite ob-vious, even to my child's eye, that the toffee, made from brown sugar and water, was allowed to set in the tin bath the family washed in and which had a nasty gray rim round the top.

We never owed a penny to anyone. Both my mother and my father impressed on me that nothing belonged to us unless we had paid for it. Not for us the misery of the families who ran up debts 'on the slate' at the local shops and then, when all their credit was exhausted, went hungry or had to go to the pawnbrokers from whom they were rarely able to reclaim what they had pawned: wedding rings, war medals, clocks, sometimes the man's best Sunday suit. I once remember my father coming home very indignant that a small shabby child had stopped him in Brewer Street where there was a pawnbrokers on the corner and asked, 'Mister, is our Mam in the pawnshop?'. He was not so much worried that the child thought he was acquainted with her mother as furious that he looked the type to frequent a pawnbroker's! So strong was my parents' influence on me that everything should be paid for at the time of purchase that even today I infuriate Edmund by refusing to have credit cards. Careful though they were with money neither of my parents was mean. My mother, in addition to regularly feeding several hungry children who came from the yards, would give to anyone, sometimes very unwisely and at great sacrifice to herself, and my father, once convinced that a case was genuine, would give generously both to causes and to individuals.

He ruled the house with a rod of iron and all decisions down to the smallest detail were made by him. I bitterly resented his male chauvinism and the way he barked out orders to my mother. He often found fault with things just to assert his authority. On one occasion my mother gave him a plate of steamed buttered haddock for his tea. He sniffed it, slammed the plate on the table, and growled, 'I don't like the smell of this, give it to our Olive'. Bitterly humiliated I refused the offer and was ordered to eat it up as good food should never be wasted. Good food indeed! He gave my mother the money with which to buy the groceries but all other household expenses such as rent, coal, pennies in the gas meter and my clothes were paid for by him. My mother did not have a penny she could really call her own and if she needed anything for herself she had to go cap in hand to him. I have often thought, in later years, that had she ever wanted to leave him, after one of his bouts of rage, she could not have done so as she would have been forced to ask him for the fare to her family in Portsmouth.

Occasionally my mother went out to do housework but there were only two houses she was allowed to work in and on most occasions she took me with her. One was St Nicholas' House (now an Abbeyfield Home) on the corner of Osney Lane and Woodbine Place, and the other was St Thomas' vicarage in Becket Street. Miss Lily Bird, who owned St Nicholas', and whose mother was reputed to be a member of the Barclay banking family, wore a navy blue nun's habit and veil with an enormous silver cross and chain. She invariably carried a black silver-topped walking stick not so much, I suspect, to aid her walking, as to swipe our legs with when we got in her way. The wall of her house was a favourite target for our grafitti but nothing more objectionable than 'Lily Bird, Silly Bird, why don't you fly away?'.

Although I was baptised by Father Robert Birley, adored by his parishioners and later to become the Bishop of Zanzibar, the vicarage when my mother worked there was occupied by the Rev E.O. James and his charming wife Clarissa. Father James was an austere intellectual man, neither understood nor liked by the people in the parish, but Mrs James was a delightful character. She wore make-up, which was not usual in St Thomas' and not entirely approved of, eccentric clothes with rows and rows of beads and her hair arranged in a very different style from the severely scraped back style of most of the godly of that period. I loved her and she was very, very kind to me. She spent many hours while my mother worked telling me stories of foreign countries she and Dr James had visited; she opened up before my eyes a world I never knew existed. They spent frequent periods abroad and she never came back from one of these trips without a present for me: a sprig of an olive branch from France, or a beautifully painted, plaster statue of the Mother and Child from Spain which I have to this day. Their only child was a son Basil, who was a few years older than me, and who was at boarding school. When he was home on holidays I was invited most days to play in the vicarage gardens with him and have tea. He had a pet rabbit which he entrusted to my care when he was at school.

What I remember most of my surroundings at home was the drabness of it all which probably explains my present taste for bright colours and jewellery (I used to daydream about being left a fortune by some unknown benefactor but this dream was clouded by the fear that I would receive the money on a Thursday and since that was early closing day in Oxford I would be unable to indulge immediately my passion for finery). My father's almost phobic feeling for hygiene was the dominant feature of our flat and there was little colour to enliven it. He firmly believed that carpets and rugs harboured germs and the floor covering throughout was linoleum, washed every day, and polished once a week. The table in our living room had American cloth nailed to it and was washed after every meal. When visitors came a snowy white, lace-edged linen cloth was thrown over it and this transformed the whole room. In my early childhood dark green alternating with plum red, chenile cloths with tassles and bobbles hanging from them covered the table between meals and there was a matching pelmet hanging from the mantelshelf, but in later years Dad decided that these too harboured germs and they were disposed of. My father, aided by one or other of his brothers, did the decorating with materials Christ Church paid for but, unfortunately, did not choose. The lower part of the walls, up to about 4ft. from the floor, was covered by a varnished washable brown wall paper with a wood grain pattern on it which Dad fondly believed gave it the appeareance of a baronial hall, but which only added to the general gloom. For economic reasons the lights were never lit until it was almost dark and it was all unutterably depressing. No animals were allowed inside the house (Basil's rabbit was cared for at the vicarage) as they, too, were germ carriers, and many years later in 1945 when my four-month-old first son contracted meningitis my father added to my misery and desperation by accusing me of being responsible for Andrew's illness. He maintained that the baby had caught the disease from my mother-in-law's dog and that I should never have taken him to visit her.

My clothes were of good quality but had enormous hems which I hated and I swore that if I ever had daughters they would never be subjected to the same indignity. When my mother took me to buy shoes my father always accompanied us for he was insistent that they fitted properly. When I was eighteen-years-old and I bought my first pair of high heeled shoes he took one look at them, snatched them from my feet and threw them on the fire. Although I was speechless with fury at the time I have since learned to be grateful for this concern of his for, unlike so many other women of my background, I have not suffered the painful consequences of ill-fitting shoes. Not for our family the joy and in-fighting of St Thomas' jumble sales for they were forbidden territory and my shoes were bought at Freeman Hardy and Willis in Queen Street and my clothes from Cape's or the SPQR in St Ebbes. The SPQR was marginally more expensive than Cape's so that although its initials stood for 'small profits, quick returns' the kids in St Thomas' always translated them as being 'Silly people quickly robbed'!

My two sons were brought up in the advertising era when Friday night was Amami (shampoo) night but for me Friday night was de-lousing night, and I was brought up in the sure and painful knowledge that each Friday I would have to endure this painful operation. Why it was always Friday I don't know unless it was to ensure that I was completely clean for the weekend and would go to church on Sunday with a clean head as well as a clean heart, but oh, the remembered agony of it. A large piece of brown packing paper would be spread on the floor and while I knelt in front of it my father would force my head down while my mother scraped through my thick curly hair with a large, but narrow-toothed, steel comb. Only when they were sure that all the offending lice had been caught and the nits dislodged would I be released to have my hair washed in disinfectant, an evil smelling carbolic. My head used to be so sore that when I got re-infected on returning to school the following Monday I dared not allow myself the luxury of scratching. Oddly enough, perhaps because we were all in the same boat, there was no stigma attached to de-lousing and any friend who happened to call on me while this was being done would eagerly offer to help and was disappointed to have the offer refused. I remember one unimaginably filthy child from one of the yards brightly volunteering to my parents the information that 'My Mum says its the clean heads what gets the lice'.

All his life my father held strong socialist views but during my early childhood he never joined a political party nor a Trade Union probably because he was afraid of losing his job as so many others had done. Moreover, when in 1922 at the age of four and wearing a starched pinafore and button boots I was taken off by a neighbour 'Logic' Nobes, who may not have had a job to lose, to one of Frank Gray's open air election meetings at the corner of High Street and Hollybush Row, he was absolutely furious and forbade me to join a joyous band of children rushing round the parish singing 'Vote vote vote for Frankie Gray [Liberal candidate], Who's that knocking at the door? If its old Captain Bourne [Conservative candidate], he'll stand there and blow his horn, but he won't do nothing for the poor'. Whatever inhibitions my father had about publicly declaring his socialist sympathies he was quite open about his strong anti-monarchy feelings and he refused to stand when the national anthem was played. What was even worse and caused us immense embarrassment and discomfiture was that if he happened to be standing when the strains of 'God save our gracious King' started up he would promptly sit down! Many years later I once heard him cynically remark that when Oxford turned Labour the rest of the country would already be communist, a view which was disproved in 1966 when Evan Luard became Oxford's first Labour MP.

Although brought up in a God-fearing household and sent regularly to church with his brothers and sisters my father was equally nonpractising as far as religion was concerned. His faith was very much based on the Old Testament philosophy, 'an eye for an eye, a tooth for a tooth' and very little 'turning of the other cheek'. Although I saw no evidence of racism in him he was decidely anti-Catholic and if I played with any Catholic children, and there were quite a number in St Thomas' because of its Irish and Italian families, this was frowned on but not forbidden by him. He saw the increasing involvement of St Thomas' Church with the Oxford Movement as a very dangerous step and regarded High Anglicans as more Roman than the Romans. Although he sang in the choir until he was married I never remember him going to church except for funerals and weddings. The Sisters of Mercy from St Thomas' Convent, where my mother was raised, were regular visitors in the parish and gave great practical as well as spiritual comfort to the poor, but they only visited our home when they knew my father was out. Whether, before my birth, he had made it clear that he did not want their charity or their spiritual guidance I don't know but he certainly lacked the courage to tell Mother Anna Verena that he did not want her as my godmother and I was frequently summoned to the convent to receive my Christian instruction at her hands. I do not know either whether it was at the Mother Superior's insistence that my mother went to church on Sundays and most Saint's Days and was allowed by my father to take me with her. I felt stifled by religion. There were so many paintings and crucifixes with a bleeding Christ depicted on them that I shut my eyes in church for most of the time, in case I fainted. The melancholy procession round the Stations of the Cross on Good Fridays was a nightmare for me. I was taught to say every night 'Now I lay me down to sleep, I pray the Lord my soul to keep. If I die before I wake, I pray the Lord my soul to take'. This prayer, coupled with the instruction to place my hands across my chest in the shape of a cross in case Jesus took me in the night, often made me too frightened to close my eyes.

My father put up a fight against my godmother's wish for me to be confirmed at the age of eleven, believing that I was too young fully to understand participation in the Communion Service but, not surprisingly, she won. A great deal of the preparation for my Confirmation she undertook herself and I was told by her in advance of my first Communion that I must be scrupulously careful to have a clean mind as well as clean hands when I partook of Christ's body and blood. I lived, quite literally, in a state of terror before the service for fear I should get a speck of dust from the prayer book on my hands or that a wicked thought should cross my mind. Such was my fear that before I received the Sacrament I dropped in a dead faint at the altar and had to be carried out of church by my brother. Jesus Christ said, 'Suffer the little children to come unto me', but I am sure He did not mean at such a cost.

I suspect that my mother stood in rather greater awe of the Church than she did of God and often my behaviour in my adult years caused her great concern. Once when I was involved in a national demonstration for nuclear disarmament she remarked to a neighbour, but significantly not to my father, who would have been unsympathetic to her view, 'I don't know what gets into our Olive at times. All this marching up and down the country. We brought her up right and I don't know what the Vicar would think of her now'. It would have been useless to tell her that the Aldermaston Marches had several bishops, and many priests on them and that they were led by no less a person than a Canon of St Paul's Cathedral but it was our church, St Thomas' Church, which mattered. In fairness to my friend of half a century, Canon John Lucas, who was the Vicar of St Thomas' at the time, I must say that although he may not have been a 'unilateralist' he certainly did not disapprove of my involvement with the peace movement. Poor Mum, for a person of her background, comformity was probably the only way of preserving her dignity and I am very thankful she did not live to see the day I was arrested on an anti colour-bar vigil, packed into a Black Maria, and, subsequently, brought to trial. I think the attendant publicity would have been too much for her to bear.

My relationship with my mother was also a complicated one. As a small child she was, for me, the unfailing source of all love, comfort and security, but as I grew older I began to get irritated by her humility and her unquestioning acceptance of the station to which God had called her. It was when I was about seven or eight years old that my attitude towards her subtly changed and I, too, began to think of her as one of the world's unfortunates. I had been reading some Victorian melodrama about an orphaned child and suddenly a terrible thought crossed my mind. 'Mum, is your father dead?'. 'Yes, dear, he was killed when I was only a few years older than you'. 'Mum', with increasing panic, 'is your mother dead too?'. 'You know she is Olive, she died a few years ago'. 'Oh Mum', I sobbed, 'Did you know you were an orphan?'. 'Blessed are the meek', the Bible tells us, 'for they shall inherit the earth'. In a material sense my mother inherited nothing and left little (I still wear her wedding ring) for anyone else to inherit but I remember her as the best person I have ever known, and her goodness lives on in other people's memories. During her lifetime, with the exception of my father's two sisters who looked down on her as 'a kid from a home', everyone loved her. In the spring and summer the depressing atmosphere of our house was transformed by armfuls of flowers which were brought by neighbours from their gardens and allotments as a 'thank you' for many kindnesses she had shown them and because they knew she loved flowers. She must have been a very pretty girl when my father married her; only 4ft. 9″ tall, slim, and with the small hands and feet of her Portuguese ancestry. Later on she became plump but never fat. She laughed a lot when my father was not around and I often wonder how different she might have been had she married someone else. Many people today, twenty-five years after her death, remember her vividly. 'She was a lovely woman, she was so kind'. 'She had the most beautiful eyes I have ever seen'. 'Her smile used to light up the whole room'. Compliments, probably because I was never paid any as a child, tend to make me feel uncomfortable and, on the whole, I tend to distrust them, but there are two which remain very close to my heart. Some years ago Father Lucas said to me, 'You have a smile just like your mother's which warmed and comforted me when I came as a very young man to be curate at St Thomas'. More recently, after I had been playing with my grandchildren, Edmund said in an amused voice, 'You think you are exactly like your father, but there is much more of your mother in you than you realise'. I can't believe that either of these statements is true but it is very comforting that Edmund and John Lucas can see any similarity between me and my mother.

The times when I saw my mother in a very different light from the mere shadow she was in my father's presence were when we went down to Portsmouth every summer for a week to visit her family. There was great excitement for weeks beforehand. All our best clothes were washed and pressed and, together with little presents for her nieces and nephews, packed into an oblong shaped rush basket with leather straps round it. When the great day at last dawned my father would bid us goodbye as he set off for work and we would walk, sedately and unaccompanied, to Oxford Railway Station carrying the basket by its straps. At least, my mother in her best navy gabardine suit and wide-brimmed flowered hat would walk sedately and I, in a straw hat and white cotton dress, would hop, jump and skip at her side. All the neighbours would turn out to wave us goodbye with a fervour which would have done credit to an arctic expedition or an african safari. I loved the hiss and steam of the train and, much to my mother's displeasure, after we were comfortably seated in our third class carriage with our rush basket safely on the luggage rack, I spent many happy hours making the fingers of my white gloves black by drawing them along the window ledges. We stopped at almost every station and when we got to Fareham the excitement was intense as we knew we were almost there. Only one thing dimmed my pleasure and that was when the ladies and gentlemen in our carriage, who always talked to me and sometimes gave me a piece of chocolate, bade us a polite goodbye as they alighted at their various stations. I knew I would never see them again and I often cried at the loss. Even today I have not come to terms with 'ships that pass in the night'.

When the train steamed into Portsmouth my mother would be hanging out of the carriage window to spot the large family delegation awaiting us. Here her position was reversed from the one she had at home. Far from being 'inferior' she appeared very superior, in their eyes, for she was not only very well dressed but also obviously well 'set up' in Oxford. There was much kissing and crying as they bore her off home which was a tiny slum house in Edinburgh Drive off the Commercial Road, right in the heart of Portsmouth and near the docks. It was all very confusing for me, and I never did work out the various relationships in the family, but it was a warm and loving one; and even if their house did not match up to my father's standard of hygiene at least we had fish and chips for supper although my mother implored me to keep quiet about this when we returned to Oxford. She bought me a bucket and spade and religiously took me down to the beach every day because she thought it might be good for my bronchitis. The week passed in a flash and in no time at all we were back at Portsmouth Station saying tearful farewells to my mother's sobbing family. My mother was very quiet on the journey back and occasionally dabbed her eyes to wipe away a tear but once Fareham was passed I began to get excited about being welcomed back home by the neighbours who had seen us off, and after a few years I knew that when Wittenham Clumps came into sight we were nearly there. Since those days the

Clumps have always had a very special significance for me; as soon as I see them I know I am home.

When I was a child my feelings for my brother Syd were very mixed. Being twelve years older than I was he qualified, in my eyes, as a 'grown up' and often appeared to be as demanding and as dictatorial as they were. Moreover, when I was being particularly difficult at home I was constantly being reminded, not only by my parents but by my uncles and aunts as well, of what a lovely child he had been, never causing any of them a minute's worry. This did not endear him to me for it is very wearisome living with saints and I was always looking for ways and means to dislodge his halo. I remember on one occasion, when he was in his very early teens, looking angelic and swinging the censer at High Mass at St Thomas', I stuck my foot out as he slowly processed down the aisle and tripped him up. I had one moment of pure delight as he lay sprawled out and crimson faced while the procession came to an astonished and abrupt halt, and then was consumed by a terrible fear that I had been guilty of nothing short of blasphemy and would most surely be consumed by hell fire. On another occasion he paid me a penny a day for a week to eat his daily spoonful of Cod Liver Oil and Malt, as well as my own. At the end of the week, having cunningly spent my ill gotten gains first, I reported his dereliction to our parents. Again my joy was short lived; he had to endure a double ration of the hated brown fishy substance, but I was thrashed and deprived of my pocket money for a month.

I don't think it was in Syd's nature to bear malice and although he often ticked me off for being cheeky, which I undoubtedly was, he showed great concern when I had one of my bronchial attacks, or had some childish ailments like measles or chicken-pox. Until I was about six-years-old I slept in a small bed in the corner of my parents' bedroom and when I was ill he would spend hours sitting by my bed reading to me from books he had bought specially for me. I can remember those books now: lovely, shiny new ones not at all like the tattered ones we had at school. One Easter he bought me the largest Easter Egg I had ever seen; it stood about two feet tall and was decorated with a most beautiful spray of spring flowers in pink, white, yellow and green icing sugar. I think if the decision had been left entirely to me I would never have eaten it, but my friends' loud clamouring for 'Just a little bit' outweighed my aesthetic appreciation and, after a day or two, it was sharply tapped with a knife and greedily devoured.

As I grew older I worshipped Syd for he was the most glamorous person I had ever known. Although not very tall he was very good looking, slim with dark curly hair and beautiful dark-lashed grey eyes. Comparing him with Syd I never saw the appeal of Rudolph Valentino. He was popular with everyone and girls used to compete for his attention. He told very funny stories and played brilliant football for

the Oxford City Football Club at the White House Ground. I was
never tired of listening to stories of the 'famous' people he met as a
reporter on our local paper. It took my breath away when he talked, in
such easy terms, about meetings with illustrious personages like Oxford's Mayor! He also taught me to dance the Charleston which was
the rage in the early twenties; I think this was for his benefit, rather
than for mine, as he needed an uncritical partner to practise with but
half a century later when the Charleston was back in fashion I
astonished my family and amazed my friends at my expertise in this
intricate dance! In my teens the age gap seemed to disappear
altogether and we became great friends – a friendship which lasted until his death, which devastated me, in 1971. Not long before he died he
remarked in a rueful voice, 'In the good old days you were known as
Syd Cox's sister, now I am known as Olive Gibbs' brother'.

3 · SCHOOLDAYS

I was sent to St Thomas' School nursery at the age of two and a half years. At the turn of the century the Fisher Education Act empowered Local Education Authorities to provide nursery education for children from the age of two years. In St Thomas' we all went to school when we reached the age of three years; in fact all the schools in south and west Oxford, New Hinksey, South Oxford, St Ebbes, St Thomas' and West Oxford, had nursery classes and, so common was the practice of taking children into these classes at the age of three, it wasn't until I was eleven years old and at Grammar School that I realised, with some astonishment, that the compulsory school age was five years not three.

The headmistress of the Infants' School, Miss Haithwaite, a formidable lady, agreed to take me in six months earlier than usual, because she had been persuaded by my parents that I was a nuisance at home and needed discipline. So at this incredibly tender age I passed through the door which had engraved on the stone work above it 'Babies' (this sign is still there today) and embarked on the so-called happiest days of my life. It is just as well that they were not to prove my happiest years for I hated school from the day I first went to the day I left at the age of sixteen years.

I think what I disliked most was being organised. Years later, when I was at Milham Ford School, I was told by one irate mistress that I had no '*esprit de corps*' and when I replied indignantly that I did not expect to go through life in a team she gave me a detention which meant school on a Saturday morning. When in 1972 I was Chairman of the Oxford Education Committee I was at a prizegiving at Milham Ford and was described by the headmistress as one of our most 'distinguished ex-pupils'. I grinned to myself and thought: 'Little does she know that I was already distinguished when I was there by reason of the fact that I was the only girl in the school to have thirty-seven successive detentions – that meant school on Saturday morning for the whole school year'.

Teaching, then, was very much the art of telling us what was what and refusing to allow us to query any of the things we were told. At primary school, and it was very little better at secondary school, we were regimented and marshalled in a way which would have done credit to a crack British military unit. There was no talking (except by the teachers) in classrooms or in corridors and most of the pupils were docile and submissive. I was neither docile nor submissive and, from time to time, created my own diversions. At the age of three years I was already in trouble. In the afternoons the toddlers were settled down on tiny canvas beds in the classroom for an afternoon sleep. Our teacher, Miss Carr, when she was convinced we were all soundly asleep, would slip off to the staff room for a well earned cup of tea. Poor

My paternal grandparents, Lazarus and Annie Cox

My mother and father, Lazarus and Mary Ann Cox

Osney Lane, St Thomas' in 1915, with my birthplace, Old Christ Church Buildings
on the right and my first school, St Thomas' Church School on the left. Both buildings
still exist, but New Christ Church Buildings (left background) were pulled down ten
years ago. *Photograph, Bodleian Library*

trusting woman; the fact that my eyes were tightly shut did not mean I was asleep and when she had left the room I went round pinching all the other children until they woke up and created an alarming row with their howling. By the time Miss Carr heard the noise I was back in my bed, with my eyes closed, pretending to be asleep, and she praised me while reading the riot act to the rest of them. It took her three days to discover the truth of the situation and when she did it was reported to Miss Haithwaite who threatened to stick one of her hat-pins in me if I ever did it again. That was obviously the discipline I needed for I never repeated the exercise. But on another occasion when one of the girls had an epilepctic fit and I fainted Miss Haithwaite threatened me with the hat-pin again because she did not believe I had really fainted and I was bitterly resentful at the injustice of the accusation! I once heard her describe me to a junior teacher as a 'very modern miss' and this frightened me even more than the hat-pin because I did not know what it meant and I worried in case I had yet another vice which even my parents had not suspected me of.

School at St Thomas' began and ended every day with a religious assembly which the Vicar attended as often as possible. He visited the school almost every day and on the major Saints' Days we all went off to church in classes accompanied by our class teacher. I am not oppos-. ed to regular instruction in the three 'Rs' but education in St Thomas' was devoted almost exclusively to these three with the addition of an extra 'R' – Religion. I get very cross these days when I hear people, who should know better, say that music, drama and art are educational frills because for me they are an essential part of any child's education and his or her later ability to live a full life. Except for singing hymns, maypole dancing on May Day, and the school pantomime at Christmas there was very little in the way of arts for us. There were no children's paintings displayed in the classroom for we never did any and the walls were covered with maps of the world, religious pictures and tracts. But we did grow things: mustard and cress on pieces of flannel and hyancinth bulbs in jam jars.

The school day was from 9 am until 4 pm with a two hour break for dinner, which we all went home for, and a fifteen minute play-time in the mornings and afternoons. During these breaks we were let loose in the school's tarmac playground. The girls played hopscotch, skipped and bowled hoops; the boys kicked a ball around, played conkers in the autumn, but most of the time wrestled or fought with one another. Our lavatories were at the bottom end of the playground: they had an evil smell and invariably froze in winter. Sometimes when it was very cold, however great one's need, it was a real effort to put one's hand up and say, 'Please Miss may I leave the room?' and more than one poor child was known to leave it too late on occasions. There were other minor excitements too; during very wet weather Miss Haithwaite would often sail into the classroom and disrupt the lesson with the barked command 'Will Emily Simmonds, Charlie Simmonds, Freddy Morgan, Chrissy Maisey and Cicely Wilkins go home at once'. These children all lived in Lower Fisher Row and the ground floor of their houses frequently flooded. When this happened they had to rush home and help their parents carry the furniture upstairs. Heaven knows how they managed to cram it into the small upstairs rooms let alone find a space to sleep in at night. I was very envious that they managed to escape, even for a short while, the boring monotony of school lessons and once remarked to my mother that I wished we lived in Fisher Row. 'You naughty wicked ungrateful girl', was my mother's horrified response, 'You just don't know when you are well off' and then added, 'the poor things'.

In retrospect I believe all those women who taught us were saints. I find it difficult to understand why, if they had any choice at all, they chose to teach in that kind of school but two or three years ago I had a letter from one of them asking if I could spare the time to go and see her. Her name when she taught us was Miss Shurrock and I remembered her as a delicate blue-eyed golden haired girl with a soft voice which she never raised. She wore lovely clothes and I thought she was the most exquisite creature I had ever seen. In response to her letter I went over to Stonesfield where she was then living and found her in very poor health having just recovered from a stroke. She thanked me for coming and explained that having seen my name in the paper she had written on impulse because she had an irresistible desire to re-live again her memories of St Thomas' of over fifty years ago. We talked for hours, with her husband solicitously hovering in the background, and she told me how, coming from a comfortable middle-class home herself, she was appalled at the poverty in St Thomas' and how upset she was to see small children coming to school hungry and in rags, and to witness their mothers' constant fight to keep the family's head above water. She remembered almost all the children by name and wanted to know what had happened to them; she wept when I told her of the horrible death of Cyril Dean in the war. 'You were a great comfort to me', she confided, 'for I always knew you were a survivor and in any case your mother was a wonderful woman'. I asked her why she had stayed there for so many years and she admitted that after the first term she wondered whether she could stand it for longer than a year but as the weeks went by a bond was forged between her and the most wretched of the children and she knew she could not leave. Those teachers were indeed saints.

I never had any trouble with lessons and was always top of the class, beating the boys as well as the girls and winning prizes as diverse as the Bishop of Oxford's prize for religious knowledge and a prize for being the most popular girl in the school. It would be more in keeping with my character and with the tone of this book to be able to say that I won the latter by issuing dire threats to those who did not intend to vote for me but that would not be true. For some reason the other kids really did like me. Perhaps it was because even in those early days I was a strong, though subconscious believer in the rights of women and the equality of the sexes. This was no doubt influenced by my experiences at home and I fought like a tiger to ensure that the boys did not exert any authority over me or over any of the other girls. The natural leader of the boys was Ron Faulkner (whose parents kept the shop in High Street St Thomas which I earlier likened to Harrods!) and, when we were choosing sides for games or sometimes less peaceful pursuits, he would be the leader of one mixed gang and I was the leader of the other.

At eleven years old some of us took the scholarship examination. This differed in several important aspects from the 11 plus examination which was introduced in the Butler Education Act of 1944. It was far more selective than the 11 plus examination which, heaven knows, was selective enough. Not all children of eleven took the examination which had papers on general subjects: Arithmetic, English, History, Geography, and a written intelligence test. Of the children taking this examination only 10 per cent were successful in gaining places at one or other of the following 'selective' schools: the Boys' Central School in Gloucester Green, the Girls' Central School in New Inn Hall Street, the Municipal School in Church Street St Ebbes, Milham Ford Girls' Grammar School in Cowley Place at the Plain, and the City of Oxford High School for Boys in George Street. All these schools were single-sex schools and there were considerably more places for boys than for girls.

The compulsory school leaving age at this time was fourteen years but the two Central Schools and the Municipal School took pupils up to the age of sixteen and Milham Ford and the Boys' High School provided education up to the age of eighteen years. For the top five boys in the examination places were offered at Magdalen College School, a Direct Grant School, also in Cowley Place, and for the five top girls places were available at the Oxford High School for Girls, a Girls' Public Day School Trust school then situated on the Banbury Road.

In spite of the word 'scholarship', in all these instances only tuition was provided free and, unlike the later 11 plus examination, parents had to buy text books, exercise books, and other classroom materials, in addition to uniform which was compulsory and expensive, and sports' equipment. Moreover, they had to sign a form saying they would ensure that the child remained at school until he, or she, attained the age of sixteen. I doubt if this obligation was in any way enforceable by law but it frightened parents who, for economic reasons, wanted their children to become wage earners at the earliest possible moment. Because of the considerable financial burden attaching to scholarships very few children in the poorer areas of the city were able to take up any of the places, but my father was desperately anxious that

I should win a scholarship and was willing to make any financial sacrifices to achieve this. He believed that a good education not only governed one's future choice of occupation but that without it, however intelligent one was, an individual had no social standing, and he, I am sure, had learned this from his own experiences.

He, and his brothers, had attended John Combe's School next to St Thomas' Church and this had been made possible by the Freemen of Oxford who paid for the children of Freemen to attend school. He often told the story of how, when the weekly attendance pennies were collected, he, and his brothers, would raise their hands and solemnly and proudly chant 'Free boy, sir'. After he left school at the age of eleven he continued to educate himself by reading any books he could lay his hands on and in later years was one of the City Library's most constant visitors. Andrew Carnegie when setting up his endowment for public libraries would have been very gratified to know of its benefit to voracious and catholic readers like my father who had not the money to buy books.

Dad had been very angry and bitterly disappointed that, because he was in the army at the time, Syd had not been entered for the scholarship examination by his headmaster. It is indeed difficult to understand why this happened for he was an intelligent and conscientious boy as his later career proved. Having left school he went to fee paying classes known as 'night school' for young adults in the Technical School in Church Street but all his working life he felt educationally and socially inferior to his journalist colleagues. He should not have felt like this for I hear journalists today say, 'When I first came into journalism Syd taught me all there was to know and there has never been anyone else like him'.

My father's anxiety for me to win a scholarship made me very nervous and I was greatly relieved when finally, in March 1929 a month after my eleventh birthday, I went off with one or two others to West Oxford School in Ferry Hinksey Road to sit the examination and found it not too difficult. When the results were published during the summer term they exceeded my father's wildest dreams for I was offered a place at the Girls' High School. My father, with great good sense, declined it and said he would rather I went to Milham Ford. His reasoning was very sound in that he thought that a child from my background, the Buildings, would find it difficult enough to adapt to Milham Ford, where only one quarter of the girls were 'scholarship kids', but at the High School, where almost all the girls were fee paying, I should stick out like a sore thumb. He finished his comparison of the two schools with the following comment: 'She will get just as good an education at Milham Ford as she would at the High School; the only difference is that the High School would try to make a lady out of her and that just isn't possible'. The day the letter arrived informing me of my success was a day of great rejoicing. We had strawberries and cream and chocolate cake for tea. My father was pleased to the point of tears; my mother was pleased because my father was pleased, and my brother, if he occasionally looked wistful, was no less pleased for me and warm in his congratulations. I suspect I just looked smug!

There was more good news to follow. The LEA wrote to my father saying that as I had done so well in the examination (I came second out of all the girls entering for it) the Municipal Charities had awarded me a Nixon Exhibition. The exhibition had been founded by Selina, wife of one of Oxford's most distinguished Mayors, John Nixon, in the mid-seventeenth century, again for the sons and daughters of Freemen. Her portrait looks down serenely from the wall behind the Lord Mayor's chair in the council chamber and often I used to look at it and marvel that over three hundred years ago this liberal progressive woman had set up a Trust that would promote the educational interests of not only working-class boys, but working-class girls as well. Such exhibitions were not awarded annually but only when the Trustees considered a pupil had done extraordinarily well. My parents were informed that the Trust would pay for my uniform, sports' equipment, text books and classroom materials. My father accepted all the offers made with the exception of my uniform: 'My daughter is not a pauper's child to be dressed by Charity', he tartly informed the Education Office.

So at the end of the summer my mother took me off to the SPQR to buy my school uniform: a navy blue gym slip, at least four inches too long and therefore having to have the inevitable hated hem, white blouse, pale blue tie, navy blazer and a navy velour hat. The hat, again, was a size too big and slipped over my eyes so that half the time I couldn't see where I was going! Of all the ugly shapeless garments the gym slip must be the most hideously unfeminine of them. But I was very proud of my school uniform and the distinctive badge in pale blue, with MFS embroidered in white on it, which was sewn on to my hat and my blazer. Black stockings and shoes and a navy blue reefer coat completed the outfit. For the summer term our navy hats were replaced by straw boaters. In addition to being hard and uncomfortable, making red marks on our foreheads, these boaters were easily damaged and sometimes completely ruined by accidental or deliberate actions which caused an extra unwelcome expense for my parents. We pretended to hate them but secretly we were very proud of them because Milham Ford was the only girls' school in Oxford which had them as part of its uniform. Two years after I got there we had a new headmistress who attempted to change them to a more traditional and feminine panama hat but a near riot resulted and she had to abandon the idea.

Although three other children at St Thomas', one girl and two boys, had won scholarships that year these were only to the Central Schools and I began to see myself as a very different person from the kids whose company I had enjoyed throughout my childhood. My father encouraged me in this when he ought to have been pointing out to his insufferable daughter that intelligence is not a virtue but a gift. In any case had I been half as clever as I conceitedly thought I was I should have realised that the ability to pass examinations is not the hall mark of intelligence and certainly not of character. As it was I read far too many books by Angela Brazil who wrote in glowing and snobbish terms of the virtues of girls' grammar and boarding schools.

But Milham Ford was not the paradise I thought it was going to be. To begin with my father was quite right when he said that socially I would find the transition to grammar school difficult, for the snobbishness of children is highly developed and can be very cruel. From my very first day some of the girls shunned me as a 'slum kid' and it was not unusual for me to be taunted with comments like 'They eat off newspapers instead of tablecloths in St Thomas'. Moreover, whereas in St Thomas' I was very smartly dressed compared with most of the other children, at Milham this did not apply for the materials of my uniform were cheap compared to the majority and everything of course was much too big. I was deeply wounded but instead of retiring into my shell I became even more belligerent and was often in trouble not only with other girls but also with some of the mistresses. Nor was I anything like as clever as I thought I was for, whereas in St Thomas' I sailed through everything with very little competition, at Milham Ford even the non-scholarship girls had to pass an entrance examination and the competition was very fierce. Except for the 2nd form which took girls at nine and ten the school was streamed into (a) and (b) forms, and 3(a) which I went into was the entrance class for the eleven-year-olds who had the best results in the scholarship and entrance examinations. At the end of the first term we were again examined and a further division made. The top half of 3(a) added Latin to its list of other subjects and the bottom half of 3(a) and and all of 3(b) were spared Latin but added domestic science and biology as subjects. The raison d'étre behind this extraordinary division defeats me entirely and to this day I am cross that I can just about translate Latin inscriptions on tombstones but have little or no idea where the various parts of my anatomy are, and my marriage almost broke up on the rocks of my appalling cookery. Every year, on the results of our examinations, a modest re-streaming again took place, a few girls in an (a) form going down into a (b) form and vice-versa. I think this scheme was very cruel because only a few girls were singled out in this way and were therefore more noticeable, and because it broke up friendships made in previous forms. By the skin of my teeth I managed to stay in an (a) form throughout my school life which was just as well as my father would have been furious with me had I been 'relegated' to a (b) form. As it was I was a great disappointment to him as my school reports carried the recurring comments 'She could do better' or 'She doesn't try'. The truth of the matter was that I was lazy and would not try to do well at any subjects I did not like or wasn't good at. I was good at Old Testament and New Testament history because of my background at home and at a Church school and moderately good at history because it was interestingly taught and I had a good memory. The only subjects which really appealed to me were English and English Literature and I had excellent results in these, not least I think, because I adored the English mistress and she took a great interest in me. In my second or third year she took me and one or two other girls to Regent's Park in London to see an open air production of *As you like it*. A young actress called Anna Neagle played Rosalind and I thought she was enchanting. Our English mistress asked us on the way home whether we had noticed that she had made a mistake in one of her lines, and not one of us had, so Miss Heywood-Johnson told us that, instead of saying 'Down on your knees, and thank Heaven, fasting, for a good man's love', Anna had said, 'Down on your knees, and thank heaven, fasting, for a *rich* man's love'. The reviews were full of this the next day so we reverenced Hey Johnny even more than we had before.

In Latin and algebra I had my worst results. Latin seemed a stuffy language to me; I could not think what possible use it would be to me in the future and I was envious of the girls who did domestic science and enjoyed it so much. Algebra I never understood from the day I was first told that ab^2 equalled xy^3, and I have remained unenlightened ever since. I regret this because I am told I have a fairly logical mind and ought to have found it interesting. It may well be, as Edmund's father who was a mathematician used to say, that mathematics was badly taught in girls' schools of that period because strictly it was not regarded as a girls' subject. But the real bugbear of my life was 'homework'; I hated it and had terrible marks for my papers. There were two reasons for this. The first, and lesser of the two, was that conditions at home with one living room and unheated bedrooms were not conducive to study and secondly, and far more importantly, I was the world's greatest procrastinator. I would always leave for tomorrow what I ought to have been doing today which meant that half an hour before going to bed on Sunday evening I would, in a panic-stricken state, be doing my whole weekend's homework. I have changed since then in the knowledge, gained through experience, that nothing is really enjoyable while the weight of things left undone hangs over one. But my antipathy to the concept of homework remains. When my nine-year-old grandson said to me proudly the other day, 'I start homework next term, Granny', I could have wept for him! I have constantly spoken out against it at many Education Committee meetings. I see the force of the argument that unless a child works for a period outside actual lesson times it is impossible to assess his or her strengths or weaknesses, but for the life of me I cannot understand why, for one or two periods of a week, children cannot be allowed to do their 'prep' in the classroom within school hours.

Although in choosing Milham Ford for me my father was eschewing the opportunity of making a lady out of me there were determined efforts, even there, to teach some of us a few social graces. Deportment, it was thought, was very important for young ladies, and we had to walk up and down the Assembly Hall with a pile of books on our heads so that our shoulders would be straight and not rounded, and our heads held high! But the jewel in the crown was our elocution lessons. The Oxford and Oxfordshire vowels are very flat and, in my view, very ugly, and we were endlessly having to chant the following:

'A cat bit a cat, and the cat, tit for tat, gave the rat such a pat that it knocked him down flat'. But we were not passed 'pronunciation perfect' until we effortlessly recited 'A ret bit a ket and the ket, tit for tet, gave the ret such a pet that it knocked him dahn flet'.

There is also a tendency in the working class to pronounce a 'd' as a 'j' when it is followed by a 'u' so the following couplet, which I think in retrospect had slightly anti-semitic overtones, also had to be recited: 'The Duke paid the money due to the Jew before the dew was on the ground on Tuesday'. This had to replace our more usual 'The Juke paid the money jew to the jew before the jew was on the ground on Choosday'. In spite of my streneous efforts to better myself I should certainly not have earned Professor Higgins' approval, for however much I tried, and indeed try today, I could not overcome the habit picked up in St Thomas', of swallowing the last consonant of all my words. I still flinch when I hear myself on radio or tape, and avoid the experience if I can.

The main building of Milham Ford was at the bottom of Cowley Place, on the banks of the Cherwell and next to St Hilda's College, which quickly acquired it when the school was rehoused at Marston in 1936. By far the greater part of the school, however, including the Assembly Hall, was housed in wooden huts scattered round the playing field and the netball and tennis courts. A wooden and wire fence separated us from Magdalen College School which was also in Cowley Place. With the older girls many romances grew and flowered with the sixth form boys. Notes were passed surreptitiously through gaps in the fence and in Oxford today there are several well established marriages which developed from those early romances. But the younger boys and girls at Magdalen College and Milham Ford were almost permanently at war: the boys would stand with their noses pressed to the fence, jeering at our efforts on the hockey and cricket field and we would retaliate with a hail of gravel. Cricket and tennis were played in the summer and hockey and netball in the winter. The tennis was optional and I think a fee may have been charged for it and netball some of us regarded as too lady-like for our tastes, but that may have been a rationalisation on my part as I was far too short to be any good at it. But I took to hockey and cricket with rather more enthusiasm than I did to lessons. My team place in hockey was on the right wing as I could run quite fast, and at cricket I was better at bowling than I was at batting. The latter I owed to my father for, whereas most of the girls bowled underarm, my father had coached me on St Thomas' rec in fast over-arm bowling.

When our boys were small they refused to play beach cricket with me as they complained that mum was too dangerous with her 'body-line bowling'. Two or three years ago when, as the Lady Mayoress, I accompanied the Lord Mayor to the Encaenia garden party we were invited by the University Registrar (Bill Dorey) to join him, Mrs Dorey, and his mother-in law, at their table. When Bill and his wife later went off to greet other friends, and the Lord Mayor was similarly occupied, this charming mother-in-law, in her late eighties, leaned across the table and said, 'You look a sensible type of woman, can you by any chance tell me what the latest Test Score is?'. She was delighted when I told her what it was, and explained that I hadn't arrived at the garden party until the latest possible moment as I had been glued to the television set watching the cricket. We discussed the merits of Botham and Gowers and then wandered back to 1957 when we had both watched Jim Laker taking his nine wickets in one afternoon. I was fascinated by her detailed knowledge of the game and could not resist asking her what had engendered this passion for what is still, with few exceptions, an exclusively male sport. 'I went to a girls' school that played cricket', she announced fiercely and proudly. 'I did too, though twenty years later', I replied, so we shook hands warmly and two or three days later she sent a box of her home-made fudge round to the Town Hall for me.

My liking for cricket and hockey was only matched by my dislike for PE (Physical Education) which I hated. This we, or rather I, endured in the Assembly Hut which, after morning assembly was over, was set up as a gymnasium. I was very slight, many inches short of 5ft and underweight, and for the life of me I could not get over that damned 'horse', and climbing ropes left red weals on my palms and ankles which caused great distress to my mother when I got home. In the Oxford Education Committee some fifteen or more years ago we spent many hours debating the problem facing us of girls from Muslim families taking part in PE lessons. Their faith demanded that their legs should not be displayed in public but the Department of Education and Science was equally adamant that 'flowing garments' constituted a potential danger when the pupil was engaged in exercises like rope-climbing or horse-vaulting. I cannot now remember how the problem was resolved but it does occur to me that few garments could have been more dangerous for these pursuits than cumbersome long gym slips, knotted round the middle with a lengthy braid girdle; but it was unheard of in those days for us to remove them and wear just our knickers or shorts. The games mistress, Miss Lamb, who wore a hideous brown gym slip and was sinewy with closely cropped shingled hair, had nothing but contempt for me, but I did not care, for I disliked her intensely although a great many of the girls worshipped her.

There were no statutory school meals in those days. The girls who came from long distances – some of them from as far afield as Woodstock, Eynsham and Stadhampton – brought sandwiches or had a hot meal cooked by those girls doing domestic science, for which the charge was half a crown a week. The rest of us went home during the lunch hour which was from twelve noon until two o'clock. Until I was thirteen and given a second-hand bicycle I walked the distance from St Thomas' to Milham Ford always accompanied by two older girls – Florence Darby, the daughter of a carpenter, who was two or three years older than me and lived in Woodbine Place, and Mary Beaumont, about a year older, whose father was the Registrar in the old registry office at the corner of New Road and Bulwarks Lane. We must have looked an ill-assorted trio for Mary was Junoesque, almost 6ft and well built, and Florrie was a lovely demure kind of girl with fair plaits and an English rose complexion. They were very protective towards me and looked after me like a pair of maiden aunts. This friendship paid dividends for me in a quite unexpected way. In 1936 when Edmund's mother, who attended St Peter le Bailey Church (now the chapel of St Peter's College), expressed concern to Mary's mother, then a leading light in the Mothers' Union at St Peter's, at her son's infatuation with this girl from St Thomas', Mrs Beaumont turned on her indignantly and snapped: 'He would have to go a long way to find a nicer girl than Olive – she is a dear little thing'. Not quite the description I would have given myself but very comforting, and my future mother-in-law, although not entirely convinced, was relieved to discover that someone of Mrs Beaumont's social standing did not regard me as a complete pariah!

Most of my comments about Milham Ford have been adverse but my five years there were not completely disastrous. At sixteen I was entered for the Oxford and Cambridge School Certificate which we sat in the University Examination Schools in High Street. Unlike the present GCSE examination it was not possible to obtain a pass in one subject; the school certificate was only awarded to those who passed in five subjects and had to contain passes in English, mathematics and a foreign language. Much to everyone's surprise and to my enormous relief I passed in seven subjects, including the three obligatory subjects, and gained a credit in history, and distinctions in religious knowledge, English and English literature. I now had the piece of paper necessary for me to enter most of the professions which my father regarded as essential to one's self-esteem and life-style.

But far more important for me was the fact that in my first term at school I met Joan Smart, who was later to introduce me to my husband, and this was the beginning of a friendship which has lasted throughout our lives. Although we meet infrequently these days the great bond of affection still exists. She was, and still is, very different from me; a lovely girl and, today, a beautiful woman. When I met her, almost sixty years ago, she had brown curly hair with chestnut glints in it, a pale skin with freckles, which she hated, and lovely grey green eyes with dark lashes. She was quiet, even-tempered and not given, as I was, to swings of temperament. Underneath this calm exterior though were reserves of strength and determination which few people appreciated but which carried her through the nightmare period of the Second World War when her husband Denis was captured at Dunkirk and spent four years in prisoner of war camps in Germany. Her background, she was the youngest of a family of four girls and one boy, was a happy one. Her father, who was an undertaker, was a member of a local family who were prominent Liberals and very well-established and respected tradespeople. Her mother, Jessie, before her marriage lived in Barratt Street, Osney, and attended St Thomas' when my father was in the choir. Though so different in personality Joan and I were inseparable and although I had other friends, notably Betty Horsham and Joan Blencowe (who on leaving school married a Malayan prince and was known as Princess Bright-Eyes), there was, for me, no one quite like Joan.

I was also privileged to spend a great deal of time with her family. They lived in a large rambling house at the corner of Oxford Road, Cowley and what is now Hendred Street, and at weekends and during most of the holidays I was part of that family. I am sure they must have thought I was a precocious little brat but in their tolerant, laughing way they accepted me without question and this did much for my self-confidence. I almost became a Congregationalist at this time, because Joan's uncle (married to her father's sister) was the Rev Thomas Whately-White who was the minister at the Temple Cowley Congregational Church which we attended most Sunday evenings. It had a large, mostly Welsh congregation, for the great majority of the Welsh miners who had come to Oxford seeking work in Billy Morris's factory had settled in Cowley with their families, and we sang the hymns with great gusto, in marked contrast to the hushed reverence of hymn singing in St Thomas's Church. Occasionally, after the service, we were invited to supper at the Manse which was a great treat. I think my mother was considerably worried by these departures from the true faith and hoped my godmother would not find out about them.

I only once heard Joan's mother speak sharply to her. A tradesman called weekly to collect Mrs Smart's grocery order and as he sat at the kitchen table with her he would write down her order and after each item like 'Three pounds of Plain Flour, two pounds of Sugar' he would say 'cue' meaning thank you, so he was affectionately known in the family as 'Mr Q'. One day Joan answered a knock at the door and shouted cheerfully to her mother 'Mr Q, Mum'. Her mother eventually accepted that this had been a slip of the tongue on Joan's part, and not deliberate rudeness, but was at pains to point out that great care must be exercised to avoid hurting or humiliating people. Joan sometimes visited me at my home but not very often as we had no garden and space was restricted, but she never gave the impression of feeling sorry for me as some of the other girls did. Mum, Dad, and Syd were very fond of her and believed that she was a good influence on me.

Milham Ford also engendered in me a great love of the English language and particularly the poetry of Wordsworth, Keats, Donne and Shakespeare. I still find reading poetry a great easer of tension and, of course, it has its uses in politics for there are few things more telling in a political debate than the apt quotation especially when it is quoted completely spontaneously!

No written or spoken word about the Milham Ford of that period is complete without mention of the remarkable headmistress we had in the first two years I was there. Her name was Miss Joan McCabe and she was so crippled, by arthritis I believe, that she travelled everywhere, even in the downstairs classrooms, in a wheel chair. The fact that in those far off days it was a motorised chair only serves to illustrate how progressive her outlook on all things was. But neither she nor the chair could manage stairs and at Assembly she would painfully, but unaided, lift herself from the chair, put two sticks to the floor and mount the two or three steps to the platform. I am sure I am not exaggerating when I say I believe every girl in that Assembly Hut felt, with her, the pain in each step but her face lost none of its habitual serenity.

She was a Quaker and invariably wore a silver grey suit with a long skirt that came down to her ankles, a white blouse and a navy and pale blue tie. Her white hair was parted in the middle with a bun at the back and she had the fresh complexion of someone who spent a great deal of her time outdoors. Her features were craggy and strictly speaking far from handsome, except for her eyes which were a piercing blue, but, if beauty really is in the eye of the beholder, she was indeed beautiful to us.

The girls adored her, the mistresses more than respected her and, in spite of her crippling disability, she ran the school like the captain of a ship and there was very little that escaped her eye. She worried about me and I believe she thought my thinness and my failure to achieve, academically, what I was capable of, was due to being underfed. My mother, when summoned to the school to discuss with Miss McCabe my disappointing progress, was terrified but she was put at her ease and reassured by the kindness of this wonderful woman and in turn managed to reassure her that food was plentiful in our house.

Just before she retired, in my second year at Milham Ford, Joan

My brother Syd, aged seven, in 1913 ('I was always looking for ways and means to dislodge his halo.') and I, aged 3, in 1921

My class in St Thomas' School in 1928. I am second from the left in the front row

'Rec' gate, with St Thomas' School

With Father Arnold
Mallinson outside
St Thomas' Church,
about 1929

McCabe was awarded the OBE in the New Year's Honours List and the whole school went mad with excitement for we were overjoyed and immeasurably proud. Asked what she would like as a retirement present she said that she could think of nothing she would like more than a collection of the girls' work. Miss Edwards, the deputy headmistress, decided that every girl should attempt some contribution and the best in each form, to be judged by a panel of teachers, would be pasted in a book and presented to Miss McCabe. There were essays, poems, sketches and paintings. My modest effort was this:

Farewell to Miss McCabe, to the tune of John Peel.

> Do you ken Miss McCabe, with her charm so dear
> Who for nineteen years has been mistress here?
> But the tear drops start, for we soon shall part
> And we'll miss her bright smile in the mornings'.

Hardly poetry but, strangely, it was selected from my form and as our dear headmistress propelled herself out of Assembly for the last time she stopped her chair where I was standing at the end of the line with the tears raining down my face; then she tapped the leather bound book which had been placed on her knees and said gently, 'Don't cry, Olive dear, I have your poem'. She went on living on the Iffley Road with her sister but she didn't survive for long.

4 · GROWING UP

Life in St Thomas', and at home, changed only gradually after I went off to Milham Ford. St Thomas' School, a year or two before I left it, had become a Junior School instead of the all age range school it had been when my brother was there. At eleven years old we all went off to different schools, those not winning scholarships going to secondary schools in west or south Oxford, depending on which part of the parish they lived in. Inevitably I began to lose touch with most of my old friends.

At home, although often incensed by my father's unjust accusations and ungovernable temper, I was slowly learning to keep my counsel and avoid most, if not all, of his physical chastisement. I now went to Church alone, or with other girls on Sunday mornings while my mother went in the evening with friends from the Mothers' Union. From time to time, and always at her request, I visited my godmother at the convent. Occasionally I was invited to tea and these 'social treats', as my mother regarded them, caused me acute embarrassment because we were 'waited on' by girls who I had known at school and were now in service with the nuns. Our standard of living, for that area, remained high, and the week's holiday I had with my mother in Portsmouth was not the only holiday we had.

My father hated to be within walls for any longer than was necessary and he was out and about, in all weathers, on his bicycle, which he was still riding at the age of ninety-two. Apart from watching football his chief recreational pursuit, in common with his brothers, was freshwater fishing. I don't think he was particularly interested in the size of the fish he caught but he found sitting on the river bank, idly watching his fishing line, peaceful and relaxing. In the light of his temperament this may sound surprising but it does not surprise me for, as a small child, my mother occasionally took me to visit him at the printing works where he was employed in Cornmarket Street. I can think of nothing more closely resembling Dante's Inferno than those premises. They were cramped, dark, hot, and smelly inside and the machines, which were constantly running, were so noisy everyone had to shout to make himself heard. I can understand his joy when, in September 1932, the firm was bought by the Alden Press and his working conditions were dramatically changed in their modern premises in Binsey Lane, next to the river, within easy reach of Binsey village and a view of his beloved Port Meadow. The Freemen of Oxford had, for centuries, had grazing rights on Port Meadow and the Cox family talked about Port Meadow so proudly and possesively that, at one time, when I was a small child, I thought it was my grandfather's allotment!

In the early twenties few workmen enjoyed paid holidays but most firms allowed their employees to take a few days off without pay. My father always took his unpaid holiday on the days following August Bank Holiday so that he got a week's holiday but was only four and a half days money short. He hired a boat from the Medley Boat Station or from Pink Hill Lock near Eynsham. It was always a punt with a canvas top to protect us if it rained but we never stayed on it overnight. Every morning we cycled (when I was a small child I was on a little saddle screwed on the bar of my father's bike) to where the punt was moored, taking with us our dinner and our tea with a bottle of beer, lemonade and a thermos flask of tea. Sometimes one of my uncles, who was unemployed or between jobs, would join us and, occasionally, a friend of my mother's from Woodbine Place would accompany us on a bike hired for them by my father. Even my brother, who was not a serious fisherman and once infuriated my father by impaling an apple-core on his fishing hook, often took a few hours off to join us but he came on his motor bike. For me the first day was heavenly. I would draw my hand through the water as my father punted along, wave to people on the tow path and then, when the boat was safely moored, scamper across into the fields to pick wild flowers or sit by the river's edge feeding the dab chicks and watching the voles burrowing into the bank. By the second day these joys began to pall. I missed company of my own age and felt faint when my father caught a fish and, after taking the hook out of the poor squirming creature, killed it with a kind of wooden mallet. For my mother I think the whole week was little short of purgatory. When she had a friend with her they chatted away or took short walks along the riverside but she was always tormented by the fear that something would go wrong and it usually did. Once, as my father sat by the bank fishing, a wasp crawled up the inside of his trouser leg and, not realising what it was, he brought his hand down in an almighty slap and was badly stung. His immediate reaction was to jump into the water to soothe the pain which wasn't the most sensible thing to do as he hadn't any dry clothes to change into. We had to return the boat immediately and my father cycled home in clothes dripping with water, furiously blaming everyone but himself. I sat miserably on my little saddle in front of him, with some of the water from him dripping on to me, having to bear the brunt of his fury.

Perhaps the funniest thing that happened, although he was livid about it at the time, was when he flung his line backwards over his shoulder to get a good sweep out into the centre of the river and the hook got caught in the rear of a cow. The beast let out a surprised moo and then, still attached to my father's line, lumbered off round the field. Fishing tackle was an expensive item and my father, not wanting to lose his line, careered round the field still clutching his rod until he caught his foot in a rabbit hole and rod, line, reel, and hook were lost for ever, with Dad having only a twisted ankle for his pains. Unfortunately Mum and I burst into hysterical peals of laughter which we could not control, and to punish us he cut short our holiday by a day, not realising that this was in no way a privation for us as we were not enamoured of these fishing trips.

When winter came we were all closed in upon ourselves. Sometimes we played dominoes or cribbage but fortunately my father was a great reader. As well as his library books he had the *Daily Herald* every day and *John Bull* once a week and to our relief he would often argue with them instead of with us.

My mother and father both made much of birthdays and Christmas. This was probably because of their own deprived childhoods and they certainly spared no expense, making these long-remembered feast days which we looked forward to for weeks beforehand. We were given, by their standards, expensive presents, and always something we had been hoping for.

On birthdays we had a birthday cake and friends came in to tea (many of them were not invited but my mother could never refuse them). Christmas was a splendid affair. For days beforehand the table would be cleared and, with a pot of paste, made out of flour and water, we would make paper chains from slips of coloured paper we had bought at the Penny Bazaar in St Ebbes. We had a small Christmas tree with real coloured candles in tin-foil holders on it, but because of the dangers of fire the tree was always placed out of a draught and the candles never allowed to burn too low nor left burning at night.

When I went to bed on Christmas Eve my mother gave me a pillowslip to hang at the bottom of my bed and it was bulging with presents when I woke up, usually in the very early hours of the morning. I could never understand when my boys were young why they did not wake early on Christmas morning and they recount with great glee how, if they were not awake by 6 am, Mum used to come and wake them up because *she* couldn't wait any longer! I am delighted to learn that my grandchildren have inherited this particular weakness of mine. I cried when I was told that there was no such person as Father Christmas and resented the news for a very long time.

I have enjoyed many banquets, notably the Lord Mayor of London's Banquet in 1985, but I have never enjoyed a gourmet meal as much as my mother's Christmas dinner. We had roast goose, roast potatoes and brussel sprouts followed by my mother's rich Christmas pudding and custard. There were no threepenny bits in the pudding for my father regarded such practices as unhygienic. We were always too full to eat the mincepies so we had them at tea-time with our Christmas cake.

One Christmas, however, when I was in my teens I came home from church and the wireless was on and, just before Mum dished up the dinner, a man who I believe was called Christopher Stone made a moving appeal for the starving people of Europe. I sat there completely silent and, as my mother filled our plates, I burst into tears and said

I didn't want any food. Poor Mum, she was very upset having spent many uncomfortably hot hours preparing it, and having the cook's usual pride in a well cooked meal. When I told her why I couldn't eat it she got even more cross and said, 'Don't be so stupid, our Olive, I can't pack up this Christmas dinner and send it to Europe. Even if it ever got there it wouldn't be fit to eat'. This reduced me to fresh sobs but before I incurred my father's wrath her face softened and she said with great good sense and practical comfort, 'Come on, my duck, sit down and eat your dinner and afterwards, when the post office is open again, me and your Dad and Syd will buy a postal order and send it off'.

But my joy on Christmas day was tempered by the fact that in the evening I knew we must go off and visit my grandparents who lived in the next block of flats to ours. It was horrible; most of my grandmother's children were there together with their own children although, sometimes, having been insulted the year before by one or both of my father's two sisters, a daughter-in-law would revolt and refuse to come, occasionally being brave enough to keep her children away too. How we all crammed into that one room I don't know. The men drank beer and whisky, the women port and lemon, and ruby wine, and the children fizzy lemonade. As the evening dragged on, apart from the noise and the heat, my aunts and uncles would get quarrelsome after their drink and I often got very frightened and would begin to cry. My father, in spite of remonstrations from my grandmother, said I needed a damned good hiding, and would give me a slap round the face. But one Christmas night, above all others, stands out in my memory. I fell asleep during the festivities and was put to bed in a room where one of my uncles and his wife, who lived with my grandmother, slept. I suppose my parents didn't want to wake me up to take me home but I woke up in the night feeling I was suffocating and found myself crushed between the bodies of my aunt and uncle. They were snoring heavily and I was filled with revulsion, but I dared not cry out in case I landed myself in more trouble. There has been no other situation in my life which has repulsed me more.

I don't ever remember seeing Syd at one of these nightmare tribal gatherings but I suppose, by the time I was old enough to be aware, he was old enough to follow his own activities, though I am sure not with my father's approval.

Poor Syd, while there had been a lessening of my problems at home, as Syd grew older his increased. Always a less aggressive character than me, as a boy he had been prepared to submit to my father's will but later on Dad's persistent interference in his affairs upset him and it made him stubborn. I believe the crux came when Dad forbade him to sign the contract Aston Villa offered him as a professional footballer. I am sure my father was right in believing, at that time, that my brother's interests would be better served in journalism than in professional football, which in those days lacked the security it now enjoys; but, had he talked to him quietly about it, and not ranted and raved, Syd would not have felt cheated at missing what most young boys would have regarded as the chance of a life-time.

There was also constant trouble about Syd's courtship of a girl, Winnie Judd, two years younger than him, who lived in Summertown with her widowed mother. Winnie was the youngest of a family of five and Mrs Judd was a very strong and determined character, for it had been no mean struggle to bring her family up to the high standards she had set herself. From their very first meeting my father regarded her as an adversary, as he did anyone who didn't agree with him, and she in turn had no love for him.

In spite of the nature of my brother's work, which often kept him out late at night, my father always suspected that he was out with Winnie and refused to give him a door key although at ten o'clock sharp the door would be locked and bolted. By this time I was sharing a bedroom with my mother while my brother slept in the same room as my father. Arriving home late, and getting no response to his knocking on the front door, Syd would come round timidly tapping the windows and my mother, in tears, would beg my father to let him in, but just as I, as a small child, had to be left in a dark cupboard to teach me a lesson, so Syd had to be left outside, often in the cold, in a similar exercise in education. It was not a happy time for him and in 1927, less than a year after his twenty-first birthday, he left Oxford and took a job as a reporter on the *Rugby Advertiser*. We did not see much of him during his time there and this, I believe, gave my father food for thought for when Syd came back to Oxford at the beginning in 1929, to work for the Oxford *Mail* and *Times* (the *Oxford Mail* having been born in 1928), the relationship between them was much improved and the atmosphere at home much happier and relaxed. About this time Syd exchanged his motorbike for a second hand Bull-nosed Morris, which had a canvas hood, was painted purple, and was affectionately known as 'Pansy'. As the car-owning population of that time was not large I was so proud to have a brother with a car and when he occasionally brought me to school, or picked me up, my joy knew no bounds. We might not have table-cloths in St Thomas' but we did have brothers with cars!

When I was about twelve-years-old my brother asked, and was given, my father's permission to take me, most Saturday afternoons during the football season, to Reading, where his assignment was to report Reading Football Club matches. Oxford had no professional football club until 1947 and with this lack in the city it was important to the *Mail* and *Times* that their readers had first hand accounts of the matches played between Reading and other professional teams. Any telephones on the ground at Reading were occupied by sports reporters from the national daily and Sunday newspapers, but that was an obstacle the *Mail* and *Times* were determined to overcome in the interest of their readers, and my trips there were not joy-rides but an important, if minor, contribution to sports reporting! During the summer months Syd had been to Reading and, having found a house with a telephone, not very usual in the thirties, about half a mile from the ground, had negotiated an agreement with the owners for the exclusive use of their phone on Saturday afternoons during the football season. He covered the reserve team matches as well as those of the first team. The arrangement was that my brother would report the match and, once during the first half and once during the second half, and then immediately the final whistle blew he would hand the copy to me and I would rush off at great speed to deliver it to a friend of Syd's called Stan Huckings, normally employed in the Treasurer's Department of the City Council, who was stationed by the phone and he would read it over to the news desk at the *Oxford Mail*. Oh how I loved the excitement of it all. I considered myself very lucky to have been selected for this honour but, incredibly, I was paid a shilling for doing it while Stan Hucking received the princely sum of half a crown for his lonely vigil by the phone. I did this for two, if not three, seasons and there was no outing I looked forward to more. My mother would give me a hot dinner before we started and Syd would collect me from home and would give me a bag of Radiant toffees which he had bought at Wright's the shop opposite the *Oxford Mail*, in new Inn Hall Street. We would then go off to pick up Stan at Marlborough Road where we would all cram into the front seat of Pansy (the only back seat was the dickey which was entirely exposed to wind rain and cold) and set off for Reading singing the latest hit tunes and exchanging jokes. When we arrived at Reading we left Stan at his lonely telephone outpost and went to the ground where, after Syd had parked the car, we climbed up into the press box where I felt very important sitting in a reserved seat next to Syd. After a bit though I became so occupied with the game that I felt rather cross when he handed me the copy and told me to run as fast as I could to Stan. I became a great favourite with the gate-man and when I got back panting from my near-Bannister mile he would bring me up to date with the glorious feats of Reading's outside left whose name I cannot now remember but who was Welsh and whom I adored.

Syd was a very active member of the National Union of Journalists and became secretary of its Benevolent Fund. He raised thousands of pounds for press charities and was the organiser of the first Press Ball which became one of Oxford's most important annual social events for many, many years. The first ball was held in the Clarendon Hotel in 1930 and was attended by anyone who was anyone, including the Mayor and Mayoress! When Syd chose me to present a bouquet to the Mayoress I was convinced that nothing so important could ever happen to me again. However, as the occasion drew near I suffered an agony of nerves and tearfully explained that I could not to it. My parents, who had bought me a red velvet dress with a white lace collar for the event, were horrified but Syd suggested that Joan Smart should be invited to come with me and this invitation was greeted rapturously by us both. I presented the bouquet, performed a passable curtsey and then sat on a chair next to Joan giggling, admiring the beautiful dresses, and watching the dancers; we believed we were now part of High Society. Next day there was a photograph of me in the paper, which I carried about with me for weeks until it became so tattered it fell apart, and I was overcome by the fame of it all. Forty years later Edmund was sitting next to a chap on the bus who suddenly thrust a copy of the *Oxford Times* under his nose and pointing to a photograph of me said, 'If I see that bloody woman's face again in the paper I shall give up buying it'. So much for fame!

In 1932 Syd married his Winnie. My father, at long last realising that my brother wanted her, and would have no one else, for a wife, only stipulated that he should at least be in the position to buy a house and not live in rooms, as most of the young married couples in St Thomas' did, if they were not, in fact, living with their parents. It is incredible, in this day and age, that any father should make such a stipulation to his twenty-six-year-old son who was earning almost three times as much as his father but I doubt whether Syd was so much obeying my father's command as using his own good sense in the matter. They found a delightful newly-built, semi-detached house at the top of Morrell Avenue. It had a front and back garden, overlooked South Park, and cost £850 freehold. Dad gave my brother half of the deposit of £85 as a wedding present but I wonder sometimes whether he afterwards regretted it for immediately after they moved in, Winnie having left her job with the Oxford University Press, they bought a dog, a black and white terrier called Toby! I remember little about the wedding except that my mother cried, that there was an air of unarmed hostility at the reception which is not unusual at these ceremonies, and that as one of the two bridesmaids I wore a long dress, fit for a princess, in primrose chiffon, with a deep ruche at the hem.

There was a loneliness at Old Christ Church Buildings after Syd left and I spent more and more time with Joan at Cowley. We were now fourteen and beginning to take an interest in boys, no longer regarding them as our natural enemies but as objects of our romantic attention. I do not know how to explain the innocence of these affairs nor can I fully understand it, but it is not my memory which is at fault. Our relationships were tender with little physical expression other than holding hands and a few misdirected kisses. Autres temps, autres moeurs? Were we really soaked in Victorian values? Were we really constrained by a devotion to our parents and a happy family life? Was it our religious upbringing or was it because a less caring society did little for those who fell by the wayside? Certainly we had no television in those days and *Lady Chatterley's Lover* had not broken through the tight fist of

British censorship but, on the other hand, neither did we have sex education at home or in school and the Pill had not been invented. In my later teens, of course, I knew of several unwanted pregnancies but while I was at school I never heard of a school-girl pregnancy. I have heard too many politicians moralising on this subject to want to fall into the same trap, but looking back I suspect that our innocence was due to little more than the fact that physically and emotionally we were 'late developers'.

I did not lack boy friends for I was attractive, rather than pretty, with brown curly hair, and long-lashed hazel eyes which were more often green than brown. I had a quick wit and plenty of spirit and would not allow any boy to think he could dominate me, no doubt a consequence of my mother's experiences at home. I still have tender memories of my first love affairs and particularly of two of them.

Neville Rogers who was at the Municipal School lived in Temple Cowley. He came from a very famous Cowley sporting family and was the youngest son of 'Basher' Rogers and a very gifted cricketer. He captained his school cricket team and after leaving school became opening bat for Hampshire County Cricket Club. I was very proud to be his girl friend and to be seen in his company but no searing flames distinguished this romance. In the winter we walked over Lye Hill, chattering about everything and particularly sport, or kicked a football about on Cowley Marsh. In the summer I spent countless idle hours, chewing grass, and watching him play cricket for the school or practising in the nets at the school sport's field where St Catherine's now stands. His great friend was Bert Bray who was also a fine cricketer and an all round sportsman but Bert sustained a serious leg injury during the war which put paid to any future sport. After the war Bert became finance officer in the Oxford and Oxfordshire Education Departments and his friendship and advice during my thirty years membership of the Education Committee proved invaluable. The fact that I was a very poor second to cricket in Neville's affections eventually began to pall and the romance, if it could ever have been called that, withered away rather than died a sudden death.

But at fifteen I fell in love, deeply, completely, and as it turned out, hopelessly. There is probably nothing so poignantly sweet as memories of falling in love for the first time. He was called Nigel Gidney and was at the same school as Neville, the Oxford Municipal School, which in 1934, after amalgamation with the Boys' Central School, became Southfield School. The school's Roll of Honour contains the following entry:

Flight Lieutenant N.A. GIDNEY, RAF (30-37). Nigel Gidney has been a name to conjure with in the history of Southfield, for if ever a boy was an examplar to his fellows of the virtues one looks for in youth it was Nigel. He was a devoted and able scholar and in his work he showed something of the ease and grace that were his special marks in the realm of sport. And as a sportsman he excelled and overtopped his fellows. The speed that made him Victor Ludorum in athletics served on the rugger field to gain him many a dazzling try. He was a great Captain of Cricket, unselfish to a degree and inspiring as a fielder. That he should later play cricket for Oxford City and rugger for Oxfordshire and Gloucestershire came as no surprise to those of us who had prophesied for him international honours. As head boy he left behind a reputation that can never be excelled.

He joined the RAF on leaving school and early in the war was posted to the Middle East. Of the important work he did there we shall never hear, for, with typical modesty, he gave but hints in his letters and promised to tell us more on his return. He was shot down at Mersa Matruh this summer (1942), but his bright flame still burns in the hearts of all those whose privilege it was to call him a friend'.

But when I first knew him he was only fourteen and although with his fair hair and blue eyes he looked to me like a young Viking, he was, in fact, rather shy. He and his brother and sister lived in the school house in Garsington where his father was headmaster of the village school, and it was in the Witcombs' house in Garsington that I met him. While I had been watching Neville play cricket Joan had developed a close friendship with Arthur (really Valentine!) Witcomb and was as warmly welcomed into his family as I was into hers, and I was happily received there too. For me it was love at first sight and I pursued him with a single-mindedness, which, had it been directed to my studies, would have done me credit. I went with Joan and the Witcombs to evangelical services at Garsington Church and attended every social function in the village to which I could beg an invitation. During the week I contrived to bump into him as he cycled home from school and, shamefully, revived my friendship with Neville to obtain invitations to school functions. My persistence was rewarded and at long last I broke through the barrier of his shyness and he tentatively invited me to go on a picnic with him. My joy knew no bounds, nor did I find any reason to hide it. And in this way began the halcyon summer of 1933. It was a time of pure magic; the sun always shone and our pleasures were simple and innocent. We cycled to Wittenham Clumps through a cluster of villages called The Baldons chanting merrily as we passed through them, 'Big Baldon, Little Baldon, Baldon on the Green, Toot Baldon, Marsh Baldon and Baldon in Between'. We sat on a five-barred gate off the Garsington Road and threw stones into the brook which ran beside it. Once or twice, when I was staying with the Smarts, we met very early in the morning and went mushrooming while the dew still shivered on the grass. Wordsworth could have been writing of us, instead of the French Revolution, when he said, 'Bliss was it in that dawn to be alive, but to be young was very heaven!'.

We were deeply in love and made tender plans for what we would do when we left school. If anyone had told us of the Chinese proverb 'When men talk of the future the rats in the ceiling laugh' we would airily have dismissed it. We were different. But Nemesis struck long before we left school. I had managed to keep this association secret from my parents but when Nigel's parents learned of our close relationship they forbade him to see me, concerned that his youthful passion would damage his school career especially as I was a year older than he was. They were civilized enough, though, to allow him to see me and tell me. He wrote a farewell message in my autograph book. It read:

There are three tame ducks on our mud flat, eating and sleeping and growing fat,
Taking their pick and maybe more of the overflowing barnyard store,
But when the wild geese stream overhead, one duck remembers things past and dead,
He cocks a lazy but quizzical eye and makes a feeble attempt to fly,
He's fairly content with the state he's in, but he isn't the duck he might have been'.

I was expecting something much more romantic – on the lines of Elizabeth Barrett-Browning or Christina Rossetti – and I was very sad. Looking at it many years later I realise it might have had a significance which I missed at the time. I thought my heart would break; I couldn't eat, I couldn't sleep and I was convinced I would never be happy again. I tried to remember this terrible feeling of utter desolation when my sons had their first love affairs and would ask miserably when something went wrong, 'Any letters for me, Mum?' 'Any telephone calls?'.

Tunes are very evocative of past experiences and when I occasionally hear on the radio the strains of 'Auf Wiedersehn' which was the current favourite tune of that time I get quite a lump in my throat. I can remember the words to this day: '...I know my heart won't beat again, until the day we meet again...' My heart, of course, did not stop beating and we did meet again, from time to time, but with a coolness on my part which hid my hurt. The last time I saw him was during the war, I think in 1940 or early 41. He came into the public library, where I was then working, looking unbelievably handsome in RAF uniform and asked me out to dinner. I declined on the grounds that I was working late that evening, but that wasn't the whole truth as any of my colleagues would have changed late duties with me. The truth, I think, will reduce my present day friends to hysterical laughter. I was offended, deeply offended, because he had brought me, as a present, a box of fifty cigarettes. I did not smoke and was shocked that he thought I was the kind of girl who did!

I never saw him again and when, in the autumn of 1942, I learned of his death I shed many bitter tears; for him, for young love and for my refusal of his last invitation.

Shakespeare, describing the seven ages of man, draws a distinctive line between the various stages of life but in one's own it is a much more blurred picture and vanity plays a large part in our attitudes. I was already past middle age before I realised I had reached it and, today, it gives me a severe jolt to hear someone who is several years younger than me described as 'elderly'! Perhaps our most conscious transition is from childhood to being an adult and, I suspect, in most people's minds, leaving school stands out as the turning point. It certainly did in my case for at sixteen, because of a combination of circumstances, my whole life changed.

Towards the end of the winter at the beginning of 1934 my recurring bronchitis was replaced by a severe attack of pleurisy. The pain was intense and I had a very high fever. Steaming kettles and Friar's Balsam were banished and poultices of Antiphlogestin, which seemed almost red hot to me, were firmly applied to the affected places. My devoted Dr Thompson, now considerably older, called twice daily and, after a while, the pain subsided and my temperature returned to normal. I was very pale and weak after this illness and, for a while, was only allowed out in a wheeled chair. Dr Thompson talked, in worried tones, to my parents about my health, fearing, I think, that I might develop tuberculosis, known as consumption in our family, which was the scourge of the twenties and thirties, especially in the working classes. He talked of a long holiday, in the following winter, in a warmer and healthier place than Oxford, probably thinking of Eastbourne where, when I was a very small child, he had arranged for me to spend a fortnight with my mother in a convalescent home for poor children.

But neither he, nor my parents, had reckoned with my godmother. She never visited our home but I am convinced she knew everything that went on in it. Miss Evelyn Bailey, the 'no-boater' headmistress who had replaced Miss McCabe at Milham Ford, was well known to my godmother for she was a devout Anglo-Catholic and spent a great part of her holidays 'in retreat' at St Thomas' Convent. Mother Anna Verena, on hearing of my illness, and the advice being tendered by Dr Thompson, summoned Miss Bailey to a conference at the convent; long discussions took place and subsequently searching enquiries were made, references checked, and an offer made to my parents for me to live for a year with a professional family in Nice where I would be a companion to a girl of thirteen, the only child of the family, conversing in English with her. When she was at school I was to help with light tasks about the house. In addition to sharing fully their family life I would be paid one hundred francs a month (about five shilling a week) pocket money. In retrospect I must have been one of the original au pair girls. It says much for my father's character, and is to his eternal credit, that, in spite of the fact that most of the arrangements had been made behind his back, by my godmother, and that there would be financial implications for him not least the cost of my return fare, he did not hesitate to accept the offer. He was so concerned about my health that he contemptuously dismissed my mother's tearful protests that I might be sold into the white slave market, but concerned himself solely with how I was to get there safely. Dr Thompson's advice was sought and he suggested that, as it was now the spring and the weather was improving daily, I should sit my school certificate, spend the summer at home and, if possible, travel to Nice in the early autumn. This he pointed out would also provide the time for enquiries to be made about my travel arrangements. I think there must have been communications between Miss Bailey and the heads of other schools for, presently, I was invited to tea by a very nice family called Cooper who lived in Church Cowley Road and whose elder son Colin was participating in an exchange holiday visit with a French schoolboy from Marseilles called Ernest Dalmas. It was suggested that since Marseilles is relatively close to Nice he would make a suitable travelling companion for me. My father was perfectly satisfied with the credentials provided and it was agreed that I should leave for France in the first week in September accompanied by Ernest.

During the summer there was much feverish buying of new clothes from Cape's and the SPQR but I don't think my mother had ever been told that the prevailing climate of the Côte d'Azure was a warm wet winter and a hot dry summer for, mindful of my weak chest, she bought me clothes most of which would have been more suitable for the polar regions. Indeed I was thankful not to find a brick in the bottom of my trunk for, in St Thomas', instead of hot water bottles, we had bricks, heated in the oven, and wrapped in layers of newspapers, to warm our beds.

And so in September 1934 I said a temporary goodbye to my family and friends and a permanent goodbye to my childhood.

My very own passport signed by Sir John Simon, His Majesty's Secretary of State for Foreign Affairs, described me as a student, 4 ft 11 inches tall, with brown hair and green-brown eyes.

5 · FRANCE

We left Oxford on the 7.30 am train for London which got to Paddington at 9 am in time to catch the Newhaven train from Victoria at 10.30 am. My father and brother and a few friends saw me off at Oxford but my mother was too upset to come to the station. She was weeping bitterly at home for I don't think she ever expected to see me again. I, too, wept at leaving her, but was too excited at the prospect of the journey, and going abroad, for my tears to last long. Once the decision for me to go to France had been taken in the spring, the rest of the time, in spite of my anxieties about my school certificate, had passed in a flash. Many of my friends, particularly those in St Thomas', regarded me with some awe for embarking on this adventure and I enjoyed basking in this limelight and gave little thought to what was really involved. It hit me soon enough; the train had scarcely passed Osney Cemetery before the most terrible doubts began to torment me and the horror of what was happening suddenly dawned and I was homesick before we reached Appleford Junction. Ernest chattered happily away in his new found English but my pain of separation from home was so great, it was almost physical, and it took all my strength when the train stopped at Didcot not to get out and return to Oxford. One thing above all had stopped me and that was the knowledge that my father had spent, for him, a great deal of money on my ticket and my clothes and, in addition, had thoughtfully provided me with enough money to pay my fare home if things went wrong or I was unhappy, and I really could not let him down. Having come to that decision I was determined to make the best of the situation and get as much out of this seemingly endless year as possible.

It was a lovely autumn day; the three-hour sea passage from Newhaven to Dieppe was calm and a sense of excitement quickened in me again as we stepped from the boat into the Paris bound train although, disappointingly, I could not find much difference, visually, between Northern France and England. We arrived in Paris about 5.30 pm and had a three and a half hours wait there before catching our final train from the Gare de Lyon for the South of France. Ernest, who had been in Paris once before, was anxious to show me all the sights but after seeing the Eiffel Tower, the Champs-Elysées, Notre Dame and the Sacré-Coeur I was so exhausted physically, and emotionally, that I was grateful when he suggested we had a meal before boarding the train. I think I had an omelette and chips for I was too tired and nervous to attempt, at that moment, to adjust to French cuisine although he tried to press several strange dishes on me.

It would be difficult to imagine a more physically uncomfortable journey than travelling through the night from Paris to the South of France in a third class carriage in the thirties. But we were young and resilient and although we couldn't sleep on the hard wooden seats we occasionally dozed between stations. As we steamed down the Rhône Valley the names of the stations were pure magic, for I had only ever seen them before in my school atlas, and never expected to be passing through them: Dijon, Lyons, Montélimar, where its famous nougat was being sold on the platform, Avignon, Aix-en-Provence, and finally, terrifyingly for me, Marseilles, where Ernest was to leave me. With Gallic courtesy he placed me in charge of the guard, which he had undertaken to do, gravely bade me 'au revoir' and rushed off, with almost indecent haste, to be gathered up into the bosom of his family. I was alone; my last link with England and Oxford gone. I have never been so frightened in my life but worse was to follow.

The train from Marseilles to Nice runs along a coastline which must, surely, be one of the most beautiful in the world but during that two hour journey nothing registered with me except my misery. At Nice the guard took me to the station master's office where the Deporta family were supposed to be waiting for me but they weren't there and the station master had never heard of me! It was quite dreadful: I sat white and weeping in a corner of that office for the longest half hour of my life. The station master telephoned the Nice address I had given him but no one answered the phone and in rapid and excited French, of which I could only catch a word here and there, he and his staff discussed what was to happen to me. I did manage to understand that he thought it might be best to get in touch with the British Embassy but before this could happen the door of his office was flung open and I was enveloped in the arms of a tall, elegant, well-coiffed, well-manicured lady who wept copiously, and clasping me to her breast murmured, 'Ma pauvre petite enfant, mon petit choux, Quelle catastrophe'. She was accompanied by an equally elegant but slightly shorter gentleman, and a beautiful olive-skinned, dark-eyed young girl. This was the family with whom I was to spend the next eighteen months.

Since Monique's school English was even less advanced than my school certificate French it took some time for me to understand fully what had gone wrong. Apparently the Deportas usually spent two months of Monique's three months' summer vacation at their summer house at Juan-les-Pins on the Cap d'Antibes returning to Nice at the end of August. Towards the end of that summer holiday they decided it would be a good idea if 'la petite Anglaise' spent a week at Juans-les-Pins enjoying the sun and the lovely beach there as they never went on the beach at Nice which they considered was too crowded for comfort. A letter, which was afterwards forwarded to me from home, was immediately dispatched telling me to get off the train at Juan-les-Pins instead of Nice. In fact, because there was probably no one on the train bound for the Cap d'Antibes, it rushed through the station without stopping, as the Deporta family stood on the platform in horrified amazement and disbelief. It would, perhaps, have been more sensible for them to have telephoned the station master at Nice but we are not always at our best in an emergency and they simply rushed out of the station, piled into their Citroën and tried to beat the train as they raced along the Corniche. The story slowly pieced itself together in my mind as we made the return journey, at a more leisurely pace, to the Villa la Madone, Rue du Lys, Juan-les-Pins.

In an odd kind of way this unfortunate beginning of my stay with them probably did much to remove any of the artificial barriers of race, class and language which might otherwise have existed. I felt so lonely and frightened in that corner of the station master's office, while people talked about me, rather than to me, that Madame Deporta's immediate emotional acceptance of me made me feel wanted and no longer alone. They, on the other hand, might have felt less drawn to me had I got awkwardly off the train at Juan-les-Pins dressed in an un-suitable cheap navy reefer coat, and might have paused to wonder whether, in spite of my references, I was really a suitable companion for their much loved, and terribly spoiled, only child. Guilt, too, played a large part in this. It is an extraordinary, but heart-warming, fact that most people feel guilty when they have caused pain or offence to others even when they have been in no way, consciously, at fault. Because their letter had not arrived in time, the Deportas felt guilty that I had had this short but frightening experience and I felt equally guilty that because I had not received their letter, they had been so worried and concerned about me. The fault was, obviously, with either the English or the French postal services, but it certainly did much to cement an 'entente cordiale' between us.

I learned more, and not only the French language, in my eighteen months in France than I did in the whole of my five years at Milham Ford. When, on returning to England, I applied for a post as a junior librarian, in the public library, Mr Ernest Skuce, the chief librarian, is reported to have said in the interviewing committee, 'Miss Cox has presence – she got it in France' as though it was some duty free com-modity I had brought back! But I know exactly what he meant: the rough edges had been rubbed off and I had an assurance unusual in young people applying for their first job. Even now, I wish it were possible, when full-time employment returns, for all young people on leaving full-time education to experience a year in the 'outside world' before going into a chosen career.

I, of course, was very fortunate to be accepted into a family like the Deportas and I have remained a strong francophile ever since. Marius Deporta was a partner in a well-established firm of architects in Nice. Although of French nationality he was of Italian descent which was not unusual in Nice, where its patois Niçois owed as much to Greek and Italian as it did to French. He came from a poor family and had achiev-ed his undoubted success from a combination of natural ability and hard work. He was very proud of being a Chevalier of the Légion d'honneur and always wore its badge in his lapel. In spite of this his views were very left wing, verging on the Communist, but I think these must have been confined to his family and close friends as he was retained by the Roman Catholic Church as an architectural consultant. Juliette Deporta, on the other hand, claimed to be descended from the old French aristocracy and her family obviously believed she had married 'beneath her'. Certainly she could be very brusque, and on occasions condescending, to her husband's mother and spinster sister who lived in a poorer part of Nice. Madame Deporta was as right wing in her views as M. Deporta was left wing and quite frighteningly fierce arguments used to develop between them. It has to be remembered that this was 1934 and Hitler had come to power in Germany in the previous year and, with the assassination of King Alexander I of Jugoslavia and the French Foreign Minister Louis Barthou in Marseilles in October 1934, political tension in France had heightened, but to me her politics appeared to be theoretical rather than practised. From the moment we first met at Nice Railway Station her warmth and kindness to me were overwhelming. Her immediate impression of me with my drab and dowdy clothes and untidy hair was of 'un petit de loup' although she did not tell me this for many months. She soon took me to the hairdressers and had my hair stylishly cut and shaped, and, expert needlewoman that she was, bought material in the Galeries Lafayette in Nice, to make the most beautiful clothes for me. Later on, she seemed to enjoy joining Monique and me in English poetry readings, and was extraordinarily patient in correcting my French. With infinite tact she also guided me through the intricate task of sorting out the appropriate knives, forks, and spoons on their elaborately set dinner table. Good manners are, I believe, international and I have never forgotten her telling Monique and me that where personal needs are concerned 'je veux' is not socially acceptable, it must always be 'je voudrais', and when Andrew and Simon were young I was forever telling them to stop saying 'I want' and to say 'I would like' in its place.

M. Deporta, though less demonstrative than his wife, was no less kind, and always referred to me as his 'petite fille Anglaise'. There was a comic strip cartoon in France at that time featuring two characters called 'Marius and Olive'. Whether it was the French equivalent of 'Pop-Eye' and 'Olive-Oil' I don't know but it amused him vastly that we had a Marius and Olive under the same roof. Both he and Madame Deporta affectionately described me, referring to both my looks and my characteristics, as 'tout à fait méridionale' but I wasn't very flattered by this: when one is abroad, and especially when one is young, there is a tendency to be aggressively British!

At first Monique did not share her parents' affection for me; a beautiful, gifted, and above all, only child she had been very spoiled by both her parents, but I think even they were surprised at the ferocity of her antagonism towards me. She was very jealous and made no effort to hide it. When her mother kissed me or showed me any affection she sulked but it was her father's attitude which really provoked her. He had been in the habit of often bringing her a small present, a scarf, a bracelet or a purse, and after I arrived he brought a similar present, in a different colour, for me. I had only been there a few weeks when he had to go on a business trip to Florence and he brought each of us a beautiful tooled leather book cover; hers was blue, mine red. Monique was furious; she snatched mine and tried to tear it down the centre and when this was unsuccessful she scratched one side of my face, drawing blood. Her parents were shocked and horrified, and sent her to bed, apologising to me. A few minutes later I too went to my room and cried uncontrollably for I had been dreadfully homesick ever since I passed Appleford Junction but because of the kindness I had been shown by M. and Madame Deporta it had been just bearable. After Monique's last outburst of fury it no longer was, and I determined that the next day I would tell Madame Deporta I wanted to go home and would use the money my father gave me to pay for my ticket. As I sat on the edge of my bed, feeling I had let everyone down, the door of my room opened and Monique, in her nightdress and with a tear-stained face, crept in and demanded, 'Why are *you* crying? Maman and Papa love you much more than they love me'. Such self pity and such an outrageously unfair statement snapped my temper and I told her how stupid she was and she ought to realise their concern for me was mainly because they knew I was missing my family. I went on to ask her how she would like being in foreign country as I was, more than a thousand miles from her home and friends. The effect was immediate; she crumpled on to the bed at my side, put her arm round me, laid her tear-stained face against mine and said she was sorry, terribly sorry; she would never be horrid to me again and would I please forgive her. Extraordinary as it may sound she never was horrid to me again and there were times, I suspect, when her parents wished we weren't quite so close!

Nice had a charm and a fascination for me which was not entirely in-duced by the romantic things I had read about it in books and newspapers in England. It did not surprise me at all that it was the favoured wintering place of the aristocracy and the rich, and that painters, writers and musicians had made a permanent home in the hills surrounding it. The climate was superb; while I was there it had a brief snow shower, the first snow for over twenty years, and people rushed out of their homes putting their hands out to feel it. Its situa-tion, too, is magnificent with the Maritime Alps, dominated by snow-capped Mont Boron, as a backdrop, and with the coastline stretching to Cannes in the West, and Ventimiglia and Italy to the East. Only ever having seen the grey-green seas of the English coast I found the Mediterranean a startling blue but I liked it best at night when it looked like a sea of milk. And the flowers! Against the silver-green of the olive trees, oh the colour and abundance of the exotic flowers, the carnation being the most modest among them. We are entreated to see Naples before we die but I am perfectly happy to have seen, instead, the Battle of Flowers in Nice in February 1935.

I liked the town of Nice, too, with its wide, tree-lined avenues, splendid shops, restaurants and hotels and I was, naturally, entranced by the Promenade des Anglais, that wide elegant Esplanade with its ornamental wrought iron railing and seats, sparkling white from the sun by day, and a soft white by the light of the lamps at night. Then there is, of course, the old town of Nice, a self-contained town within a town. Surrounded by the wealthy, cosmopolitan 'new' Nice, it remains intact with its cobbled streets, old houses, small shops and craft industries. Its inhabitants, when I was there, spoke nothing but Niçoise and appeared to be a self-sufficient community, a race and centuries apart from its rich and fashionable new neighbour.

We lived in a large apartment at 31bis Avenue Villermont, a pleasant tree-lined avenue just off the Avenue Victor Hugo. I was amazed to discover when I first arrived in France that in French cities everyone lived in large apartment buildings and, with very few exceptions, the only houses to be found were in the rural areas. 31 and 32 Avenue Villermont faced one another and were in a culvert immediately off the avenue. There was a high white ornamental gate at the end, which could be locked at night, and both apartment houses shared gardens and a small 'parc'. Our flat was on the first floor, the flat at ground level being occupied by the concierge and his wife. It had a dining-room, drawing-room, three bedrooms, a study, kitchen and bathroom and was handsomely decorated throughout. The curtains were heavy and luxurious and most of the furniture was antique and very beautiful. The fine carpets they had brought back from Rabat in Morocco where, for some reason which I never fully understood, they were living before Monique was born. It was all a far cry from our flat in the Buildings, but not sharing my father's phobia for germs I revelled in the luxury of it.

The Villa la Madone at Juan-les-Pins was a house M. Deporta had, himself, designed as a holiday home. Detached, with a large surrounding garden, the bedrooms and bathrooms were on the ground floor and the living room was on the first floor. This was a deliberate arrangement so that in the hot mediterranean summer days the bedrooms, which had stone floors and green shuttered windows, were comparatively cool both at night and for the afternoon siesta. Each room of the house and this part of the villa was connected to the ground floor by a wooden staircase inside and stone steps outside. There were only two bedrooms; one of which Monique and I shared, with our twin beds covered by permament mosquito nets, but there was also a 'practical' room which had a divan in it but was used for a variety of purposes; reading, writing, sewing and playing cards. The garden had many pine trees in it as well as a profusion of flowers. There were also lemon trees and orange trees and an arbour covered in vines. I thought it was the height of luxury that in the summer we could stretch out on canvas chairs and just reach up and pick a bunch of grapes; very different from St Thomas' where one ''only had grapes when one was ill'' From the first floor we could see the Estérels those beautiful mountains where Grasse, France's perfume manufacturing town, nestles. From where we were the mountains looked purple but when I was taken to visit Grasse in the spring we travelled through forests of mimosa and sweet-smelling groves of orange blossom. In spite of the careful architectural planning of the Villa la Madone, its location left much to be desired because a main road and the railway line separated it from the beach and sea. More often than not its peace was shattered by the roar of traffic and, at night, a train hurtling through to Nice and Italy would wake one with a terrible start. I can only assume that, as Juan-les-Pins was fast developing as the rich play-ground of Europe, land values were astronomically high.

The Deportas' family life was relatively simple. They did very little entertaining at home; friends and acquaintances were entertained, often 'en famille' in restaurants and we were similarly invited to reciprocal dinners. The only exceptions to this were M. Deporta's mother and sister, Madame Deporta's sister who was the headmistress of a girls' lycée in Marseilles, her brother who was a naval captain stationed at Toulon, Monsieur and Madame Claire who were close friends, and Monseigneur Raymond who later became the Bishop of Nice. The apartment was transformed before Monseigneur came to dine, the silver shining, the glass sparkling, the furniture glowing, the linen table-cloth and napkins snow white and starched to perfection! As he entered the room, ushered in by M. Deporta, we had to drop to one knee and kiss his ring, but I was careful not to mention this in my letters home for fear my father thought I was being initiated into papal practices.

Looking back I suppose it was surprising that, apart from Marguerite 'the bonne' who came to us daily from 9 am until 5 pm, while we were in Nice we had no servants, for many less affluent middle-class families in England, at that time, would have regarded a maid as a necessary sign of their social status. But, altogether, I found French family life a very private affair, much concerned with each other, and particularly, the children. Madame Deporta was forthright in her condemnation of what she saw as indifference, amounting to cruelty, in the way the English handed their very young children over to the care of nannies, and regarded sending children off to preparatory schools at the age of seven years as little short of sadism.

Marguerite, who had several children and a drunken husband, cleaned the house, washed and ironed the clothes, washed the dishes and prepared the vegetables. Madame, herself, did all the cooking and most of the shopping. At least once a week she would go down to the little open market near the Avenue Villermont, choose the vegetables, prod the cheeses to discover which were mature and ask for her purchases to be delivered. I was shocked beyond measure that, with diamonds sparkling from her fingers, she always wore her 'pantoufles' on these shopping expeditions for, in St Thomas', it was a mark of respectability never to wear one's slippers outdoors in fact my mother would always change from slippers to shoes even to fetch the 'supper beer' in a jug. This to me was proof of what I had always been brought up to believe, that the English were a vastly superior race to any other!

It did not take long to adapt to the pattern of French family life or, at least, that led by the Deportas. Monique attended the Nice lycée for girls and was studying for her Baccalaureate which appeared an altogether more exacting examination than the English school certificate. During term time her father, on the way to his office, would drop her at the lycée at 8.30 am and I would meet her in the afternoons at 1.30 pm sometimes accompanied by one of her friends, Rose Nomdedeu. Breakfast was between 7 and 7.30 am: the usual bowl of strong but milky coffee, croissants, brioches and fruit. If we ate lunch during the school day, as distinct from the weekends and holidays, I cannot now remember what we had, but at 3.30 in the afternoons Monique and I had 'goûter', a large piece of French roll, without butter, but with a slab of dark plain chocolate and a glass of milk. If we preferred it to milk we could have a cup of China tea with lemon which Madame Deporta always took at this time. About once a month she entertained a few of her women friends to a bridge party and afternoon 'English' tea with tiny bridge rolls and gâteaux. Monique and I looked forward to these functions with mixed feelings for, although we adored the tea, we were sometimes roped in to play Bridge if the numbers were short, and we never failed to fall far below Maman's expectations. Dinner varied between 7.30 and 8 pm and was an elaborate meal with several courses: hors-d'oeuvre, soup, a dish of pasta, meat or fish, salad, fruit, cheese and occasionally pastries or petit fours with our black coffee but never puddings. In fact the 'English' pudding was the source of much amusement, and the family roared with laughter at the English habit of serving macaroni as a sweet milk pudding. I could not understand this, as macaroni pudding was not a delicacy I had ever seen on a St Thomas' table. All the dishes were served on separate plates unlike I had been used to in England, where the meat, potatoes and other vegetables were all on the same plate. My immediate practical reaction to this was that it caused an unnecessary number of plates to be washed! Most of the cooking was done in a Provençal style and, after I had got accustomed to food being cooked in olive oil, I liked it very much and have been a devotee of it ever since although I have never tasted olive oil in this country as it tasted there. Wine always accompanied the meal and Monique and I were allowed modest amounts but never liqueurs or brandy. The washing of the dishes was left to poor Marguerite to do when she came in the morning, and any tasks I had to do about the house were so light I have forgotten what they were.

I never remember going to the theatre in Nice but, from time to time, Madame Deporta would take Monique and me to the cinema. They were mostly American films being shown, and Maman had a particular penchant for William Powell and Myrna Loy! Much more often, dressed in elegant silk dresses, we would accompany Maman and Papa to the Nice Conservatoire for a symphony concert or a musical festival. Monique, herself, was an accomplished pianist. I always accompanied her to her piano lessons, and there was great excitement in the spring of 1935 when she was chosen by the lycée to play at a matinée performance at the conservatoire. The piece she was to play was Chopin's 'les trois Ecossais' and for weeks beforehand she spent almost every spare minute practising, until Chopin was ringing in our ears even when she wasn't playing. But it was all worthwhile because she gave a faultless performance on the day and got a rapturous ovation. I shall always remember her standing in the centre of the stage acknowledging the applause. She looked so beautiful: tall for her age and slim, her normally pale skin flushed with success and her lovely dark eyes shining as she gave a shy little smile directed especially at us in the front row.

Occasionally we went to mass at the Cathedral of Notre Dame de Nice but I found these services very strange. To begin with they were all in Latin but, even stranger to me, was the fact that there appeared to be no beginning and no end to the service, but a continuous performance like the cinema. At whatever point we went in, we left when that point came round again, and so did everyone else, so that there was a constant noise of worshippers entering and leaving the cathedral. It all seemed very irreverent to me and I was sure my mother would not approve.

At weekends, except for December and January which are the coldest months on the Côte d'Azure, we either went to the house at Juan-les-Pins or made trips by car to various places: Cannes, a much overrated town I thought, Monte Carlo with its 'toy' castle and 'toy' policemen, Toulon, or villages high up in the Maritime Alps. As Nice is only thirty kilometres from Ventimiglia on the Italian border we made frequent excursions into Italy but on one of these occasions the border guard looked at my passport, saw I was English, and spat at me through the open car window. It was at the time of the Abyssinian war when Britain took sanctions against Italy and feelings were running high. There was an excited exchange between M. Deporta and the guard and then Papa turned the car round and drove back to Nice saying it would not be right to expose me to further offensive behaviour.

On all these trips Monique and I sat in the back of the car chattering away in English which was not always to improve her knowledge of the language but to provoke her parents into asking 'what are you two talking and laughing about?'. What I loved best was when we were returning from an excursion into the Maritime Alps and Papa would break into an old French song and we would join in the choruses. In our songs we laughed and danced with the 'pompiers', met three captains in Lorraine while wearing our shabby 'sabots' and woke brother Jack up to ring the bell. I knew, and still know all the words of 'Au Pres de ma Blonde' but the funniest song was about 'my uncle Rudolph' and I still don't know whether it was an old French song or a thirties' skit for it went:

> Mon oncle Rodolphe avait cent deux ans,
> Il est mort dimanche,
> Mais le vieux chameau dans son testament à pris sa revanche.
> Tout l'argent que je guettais, aux oeuvres de charité,
> Moi je dois me contenter, d'un château qu'il habitait.
> Je le visitais.
> C'est un vieux château du Moyen-Age
> Avec un phantôme à chaque étage,
> Dans les chambres d'amis, il y – a des souris sous des lits,
> Si vous n'en voyez pas c'est parce qu'il y a des rats,
> Des rats, gros comme ça.

When we got to the last line we would stretch our arms sideways, as far as they would go, exactly like one of my uncles explaining to me the size of a fish he had caught!

They had planned to spend a fortnight touring Italy at Easter 1935 but because of the earlier incident with the border guard it was decided to go to the Pyrenees instead. What a memorable journey that was; we sang 'Sur le Pont d'Avignon' standing on the bridge itself, viewed with awe the vast Roman amphitheatre at Nïmes, and drove through the dry dust of the Camargue stopping now and again as the wild horses brought the car to a halt. When we reached the Pyrenees region my immediate reaction was how startlingly green it was compared to the Mediterranean coast. We stayed a day or two in Perpignan, which Monique and I had heard much about from her friend Rose Nomdedeu who had been born there, and then made the journey from the Mediterranean to the Atlantic across the five highest traversible peaks of the Pyrenees.

We stopped one night at a village which was dominated by the church of St Bertrand de Comminges, which Papa said was built at a higher altitude than any other church in France. It was a breathtaking journey, in more ways than one, for not only were the views magnificent but the roads, if they could be designated roads, wound narrowly and dangerously round the mountains with sheer unfenced drops below them and frequent unmistakable evidence of cars which had gone over the edge. When we reached Hendaye, on France's border with Spain, I was asked if I would like to go to a bull fight but I shuddered at the thought and I think they were relieved at my refusal and we spent a day sightseeing in St Sébastien instead. I did, however, say I would like to visit Biarritz, which surprised them but I explained that I had read about it in England. What a disappointment it was! Except that the sea was much rougher and the waves much higher I could see little difference between it and Portsmouth on a cold and windy day. What an opportunity missed; had I been better educated I could have asked to see the treasures of Bayonne which were only a few miles away. So many of the places we visited in the Pyrenees and the Pays Basque, Perpignan, St-Jean-Pied-de-Port, St Sébastien, Hendaye, St-Jean-de-Luz, became tragically familiar names a year or so later when Civil War broke out in Spain between the Republicans and the Fascist dictator General Franco.

On the return journey to the Mediterranean coast we took a different route, visiting Lourdes, Toulouse and Carcassonne before reaching Narbonne and turning the car in the direction of home. Lourdes upset me very much: that a place of such religious significance could be turned into a tourist attraction with hideous cheap souvenirs and expensive bottles of 'holy water', from a stream near the spot where the Blessed Virgin was reported to have appeared before St Bernadette, repelled me. And I was in no way comforted by the Service of the Blessing of Invalids. So many people incurably sick, dying or cruelly deformed, patiently waiting for the 'laying on of hands' in the steadfast belief that a miracle would restore them to full health, deeply depressed me then, and for days and weeks after. I was shocked too by Papa, who was normally a kindly man, openly amused by the ornate architecture of the Church of Our Lady of Lourdes which had been built from donations made by the 'cured' and their relatives – he said the Church did not miss a trick. I was still lost in my depression when we visited Toulouse and can remember very little about it. I think my gloom began to irritate the family for they were, after all, on holiday and expected to enjoy it which was not very easy with a moody uncommunicative girl dampening their spirits. I felt very guilty and made a conscious effort to put aside my misery and to enjoy Carcassonne whatever it was like. I need not have worried for I was enchanted by this walled, fortressed medieval city which had a moat surrounding it and could only be entered by a huge gate, which could still be shut and bolted, at the end of the drawbridge. It stood on a hill and could be seen from miles around so that when we first saw it, from the distance, it looked for all the world like a child's toy fort. Tourism had already begun to show its more unacceptable face here, too, but at least the souvenir stalls, picture post-cards and ice-creams were outside the city walls and hadn't at that time been allowed to cross the drawbridge.

Two other visits merit mention. For Christmas 1934 we went to stay with Madame Deporta's sister whose name I cannot remember but who was the headmistress of the Marseilles lycée and whose subject was English. She lived with her husband, her daughter Mireille and son-in-law in a very large beautiful house on Le Prado. It was here I first encountered complete female domination. The husband and son-in-law were pale shadows lurking in the corners of the house, speaking when they were spoken too and rarely, if ever, venturing an opinion of their own.

The only male showed any attention was the grandson Jean-Paul, four years old and spoiled beyond redemption. Papa hated it there and after a fourteen course meal on Christmas Eve he complained of feeling unwell and we returned to Nice on the Boxing Day. I suspect, and I think Maman did too, that his indisposition was not so much gastric as antipathetic, and she lectured him all the way home on his discourteous behaviour. For me it was a timely and salutary lesson that female domination is no more attractive, nor acceptable, than that of the male.

A far more enjoyable experience was when Oncle Robert, Maman's brother, took us in his boat to Ajaccio on the island of Corsica. It was on the way there that I saw, for the first and last time, a school of dolphins leaping high in the air and turning somersaults as they did so. My excitement at seeing the island where Napoleon was born was very much over-shadowed by my fear that we might be confronted by Le Spada, the notorious Corsican bandit, who had escaped capture by the military and the police and came down from the hills terrorising the island's inhabitants. So great was my fear that I was enormously relieved when we got back on the boat but I was very disappointed not to see any dolphins on the way back to Nice.

Much to Madame Deporta's pleasure my health gave no trouble at all; my figure rounded under the influence of Provençal cooking and my command of the French language showed a significant, even remarkable, improvement. Initially I had to wrestle with the 'tutoyer' distinction which has no parallel in modern English. I thought, at first, that 'tu' (you) rather than 'vous' (you) was an affectionate distinction but soon came to realise that 'tu' was a term of familiarity applied equally to members of the family, and very close friends, or to those people one believed to be socially inferior. I found this very difficult to accept and would never address anyone outside the family as 'tu'. It is most people's experience that a foreign language taught in schools falls very far short of what is required to converse fluently when one reaches the country concerned. I, like most other pupils, learned at school the french for borrowing my aunt's pen but what nobody told me, and certainly my text book didn't, was the French for borrowing my sister-in-law's pen. In French, of course, the 'in-law' is replaced by 'handsome' or 'beautiful' so that sister-in-law becomes 'belle-soeur' and father-in-law 'beau-père'. When I first arrived in the Deporta family I was fascinated by the way in which they appeared to refer, most times, to close members of the family in this complimentary fashion. I was touched by this and, determined not to be out-done in courtesy, I always referred to my mother as 'belle-mère' and my father and brother as 'beau-père' and 'beau-frère' respectively. The Deportas were completely mystified and wondered among themselves how an unmarried girl could possess such an assortment of in-laws. They were very relieved to discover the truth and be reassured that I was not a child bride! I think my proudest moment, as far as my French was concerned, was when, after I had been in France for about six months, I went to the bakers to get a loaf and the baker enquired respectfully, 'Mademoiselle est alsacienne?'. I rushed back to tell Maman and she was delighted and, hugging me to her, said, 'Marvellous, but of course it will take longer than a year to get you speaking perfect French'. I should have been warned!

The days, weeks, and months, slipped by fairly quickly. My father wrote to me every week with a short note appended from my mother, and my brother and Joan wrote at frequent intervals. I also wrote home weekly and Syd must have found my letters interesting because he wrote saying that his editor had asked if I would write a short article for the *Oxford Times* on 'A schoolgirl abroad'. I did and was delighted to receive payment of half a guinea (ten shillings and sixpence). But I never once lost my feeling of homesickness and sometimes, when I had just received a letter from home, the heartache was almost unbearable. Once June had passed I began counting the days until I would return home in mid-September. Then the bomb dropped! Just before we were to go to Juans-les-Pins for the two month summer vacation Maman took me to one side and said that they all very much hoped I would stay with them for another year as I had become very much a part of their family and she knew I was happy there. I was taken completely off guard and did not know what to say. I did not want to hurt their feelings as they had been extraordinarily good and generous to me but the thought of another year away from home was too awful to contemplate. I had never before told them I was homesick as it seemed ungrateful but now I tried to explain how much I missed my family and wanted to see them. This was no obstacle as far as Maman was concerned and she brightly suggested I spent a month at home while they were at Juan-les-Pins and then came back for another year. But I knew full well that once I got home I would never return. I wrote to my father, in some distress, believing he would order me to return in September and thought if I showed Maman his reply she would know that the matter was outside of my control. Instead my father, who was also unaware of my homesickness, wrote back saying the decision would have to be mine and that probably another year in France would be beneficial especially as I could come home for a month which would reassure my mother. I was distraught. I did not show them my father's letter but on the other hand I did not want to lie and, in the end, I explained to Madame Deporta that I felt I ought to go back to England before another year was up and start looking for a job, but that I would be happy to stay for another six months and forgo the month's holiday. Happy was not perhaps the best word to describe the next six months for they seemed endless; yet I knew that when the time came for me to go home I should go with mixed feelings and be very sad at leaving my French family. This proved to be true and it was a very heart-rending experience when I said 'goodbye' to them in March 1936. Monique locked herself in the bathroom and would not come out, but we could hear her sobs and they seemed to follow me all the way to the station. There is rarely a perfect solution to any problem.

I travelled alone as far as London but my father met me at Paddington and scarcely recognised me. I had grown an inch and put on weight and Maman had taken particular care with my 'coming home' outfit. It was very chic: a red and white checked silk dress with a light grey flannel coat and hat to match. Dad was obviously overcome at having me back and hugged me very fiercely. I talked excitedly in a garbled mixture of French and English until we got to Wittenham Clumps when an enormous lump formed in my throat. This dissolved into tears when I stepped down on to the platform at Oxford and was re-united with my mother, brother, and Joan. As we walked the short distance from the station to Old Christ Church Buildings it was like a royal progress, for the 'parish' was at its windows and doors, welcoming me home, and in our living room was a banner across the mantelpiece saying in gold and red letters 'Welcome Home Olive'.

6 · RETURN TO ST THOMAS

There had been dramatic changes in St Thomas' while I had been away. The worst yards, those between the Windsor Castle and the Turk's Head in High Street St Thomas, had been demolished under a slum clearance order and the residents sent to live in Council houses at Rose Hill and Barton where, from all accounts, they felt like Ruth amid the alien corn. Similarly some of the larger families living in over-crowded conditions in both the Old Buildings and the New Buildings had been re-housed outside the area. With the departure of these families much of the character of St Thomas' disappeared with them. In spite of their poverty they were lively colourful families, and many of the young people who went had been close friends of my childhood. Although our links had not been so close since primary school days, my affection for them remained and I missed them. After they first left, many of them paid return visits to St Thomas' at frequent intervals but we were never again all together at the same time and the visits became more and more infrequent until they ceased altogether.

Parts of the Friars had also gone and its people rehoused in Council housing on the Weirs Lane estate at the southern end of the Abingdon Road. Friends and 'foes', and occasional 'gang warfare', had disappeared simultaneously to be replaced in St Thomas' with warehouses and industrial premises, and in the Friars with vast areas of waste land which no one would develop until the line for an inner relief road for Oxford had been determined. But that issue was not resolved until almost forty years later.

Apart from the replacement of our gas lighting by electric lamps little had changed at home but since we were still not allowed to switch on the lights until it was almost dark much of the gloom remained. My mother was touchingly pleased to have me back but I constantly detected in her an apprehension that I might, by something I said or did, provoke my father into one of his rages. But she need not have worried: in the first few months I was home he was embarrassingly proud of me and from the way he boasted of me to family and workmates they could have been forgiven for believing I had been staying with the Rothschilds as an honoured guest! I missed Maman and Papa and Monique quite dreadfully and I doubted whether I would ever learn to live with these divided emotions. I wrote to them regularly, reaffirming my promise before I left, that I would return to spend a holiday with them as soon as I possibly could, probably in the summer of 1937.

I was immediately preoccupied on my return with the need to find a job for I felt my father had been supporting me for long enough. My over-riding ambition was to be a reporter with the *Oxford Mail* and

Times. Syd's graphic accounts of the places he visited, and the people he met, had fired my imagination and I had satisfying memories of the Saturday afternoons pent at Reading Football Club. I thought, too, that as the Editor of the *Oxford Times* had paid me half a guinea for my brief account of life in France I was not entirely lacking in literary talent! Dad approved of the idea but my mother, though not daring to make her views known to my father, confided in me that she thought the unsocial hours, the very nature of the work, the pubs and clubs and the overwhelmingly male company made it a most unsuitable job for a respectable girl. She begged me to reconsider the idea. Syd was not very hopeful of success but encouraged me to write to Bob Gibbs (R.A. Gibbs) the chief reporter whom I had known since I was a very small child, requesting an interview. Why he agreed to see me heaven knows for it was quite apparent as soon as I was ushered into his presence in his glass-plated office in New Inn Hall Street that he had no intention of offering me a job. It took him an interminable time to tell me of the qualities needed, which he obviously considered I had not got, to be a successful journalist and then he finally and pompously told me that it was not the policy of the *Mail* and *Times* to employ women as reporters. As tactfully as I could, because I desperately wanted a job on the reporting staff, I pointed out that they already had a woman, Miss Hilda Hughes, as a reporter. His quite incomprehensible reply to this was that she was a graduate, as though this in some way changed her sex. I was terribly disappointed at his refusal and not a little upset by his condescending attitude and about six years later, during the war, when he telephoned me at the public library where I was then employed, asking me if I would like to replace my brother who had joined the navy, it gave me a certain amount of mean satisfaction to turn him down.

I next applied for a secretarial job with Mowbray's the publishers in Pembroke Street but was no more successful, although the interview was not so bruising. They told me that they would have been happy to employ me had I had some knowledge of typing and shorthand. These two practical subjects had been taught at the Girls' Central School but not at Milham Ford where they educated their girls for the professions. The thirties was a time of high unemployement and suitable jobs were few and far between and competition for vacancies very fierce. My time in France, except from the health point of view, appeared to have been no benefit to me and I began to feel quite desperate about ever finding congenial work. I did consider nursing but with my weakness for fainting at the sight of blood I had not the courage to face up to it. Joan was happily working in the bookshop of F.A. Wood (now Blackwell's paperback shop) at the corner of the Turl and Broad Street but I lay awake at night unhappily aware that, at the age of eighteen, my father was still supporting me. I seriously considered whether I should follow the example of most of the girls in St Thomas' and apply for a job at Morrell's Brewery (where I should have to wear clogs!) or at the 'Jam Factory' (Frank Cooper's of Oxford Marmalade fame) at the corner of Park End Street and Hollybush Row. I tentatively suggested this to my father and he was absolutely furious, shouting that this was not what I had got my school certificate for and that a few more weeks or months of keeping me were not going to cause him financial ruin. Fortunately it did not prove to be months or even weeks for on the following Friday an advertisement appeared in the *Oxford Times* inviting applications for the post of a junior library assistant at the Central Library in St Aldates; no applicant without a school certificate would be considered. I applied, was interviewed by members of the Library Committee, including Lady Townsend (then Alderman Mrs M.G. Townsend) and Alderman Mrs Prichard, and was chosen. I have no doubt that my school certificate distinctions, in English and English Literature, stood me in good stead but that it was my time in France which was the determining factor.

My salary, paid monthly, was beyond the dreams of avarice, £60 a year. This meant that after deductions for insurance, superannuation contributions and membership of NALGO (National and Local Government Officers' Association) I took home four pounds a month. When I proudly arrived home with the first four pounds I was horrified to be deprived immediately by my father of three pounds of it for my 'board and lodging', leaving me five shillings a week for all my personal needs including my clothes. I protested strongly that not one of the other girls at the library had to hand over this percentage of her salary but my father would brook no argument. He explained that it cost fifteen shillings a week to keep me and that was what I would pay, not a penny more and not a penny less; for I had to learn to pay my way in life. In fact, for all the time I lived at home, he never did charge me more than the fifteen shillings although with annual increases in salary as well as promotions I was earning far more than he was before I was twenty-one years old. Many years later I attempted to persuade him to allow me to make him an allowance to eke out his old age pension, pointing out that he had made many financial sacrifices for me, but he was adamant in his refusal. 'You owe me nothing, our Olive', he said. 'Children don't ask to be born; they are either born as the result of a deliberate policy or as a mistake and in each case the parent is entirely responsible for the child and the child owes the parent nothing', and then he added, 'And don't you forget that where your two boys are concerned'. It really was a quite extraordinary philosophy for someone of his generation and his background.

Although I think a small part of me will always regret that I did not become a journalist, I loved working at the library and spent eight happy years there only leaving a few weeks before my first child, Andrew, was born in October 1944. The library building was at the corner of St Aldates and Blue Boar Street where the Oxford Museum is now housed, and the conditions were dark and cramped. Three-quarters of the library lending stock was shelved in the basement and this entailed endless journeys up and down an iron spiral staircase. The main lending library and the children's library were on the ground floor and sandwiched between these was the newspaper room where the daily newspapers were secured to boards on the wall and anyone wishing to read or study them had to stand to do so. It was a a smelly, horrible place, especially in wet weather, and the caretaker had to spray it several times a day with a 'disinfectant gun'. On the second floor, reached internally by a wooden stair-case and externally by a steep flight of stone steps, was the reference library. This was a dark, but beautifully panelled and proportioned room, with reference books and periodicals. There were splendid highly-polished tables at which readers could browse through volumes of the *Encyclopaedia Britannica* or the *National Geographic Magazine*. Branching off the reference library were several small alcoves which could be 'booked' in advance, but without charge, by students of any type, for individual study. Above the reference library, after another interminable flight of wooden stairs, was the secretary's office which, at best, could only be described as an attic. In those days NALGO was no more than a periodic gathering of socially minded members, for no self-respecting Trade Union would ever have allowed the secretary, Miss Mitchell, to work under those conditions and to have to negotiate those stairs every time Mr Skuce summoned her to his office. The only lift was a book-lift operated by rope hand-pulleys.

When I first joined the library the staff, except for the city librarian, Mr E.E. Skuce, was entirely female although by 1939 we had three male librarians. But to begin with there were Mr Skuce, the deputy librarian Miss M.C. Campbell, and nine young women ranging from sixteen to twenty-five years. They were known as librarians or library assistants depending on whether they had qualified under the Library Association examinations. Two of the girls had been at the Girls' High School and the other seven were from Milham Ford. Taken as a whole they were unusually good-looking girls and were known in the city as 'Mr Skuce's young ladies'.

Mr Skuce, who joined the library staff at the age of fourteen years, was a pompous ass, over-preoccupied with detail. One of my jobs as a junior was to make his tea and he was always admonishing me for not 'warming the pot', although I invariably did and was quite sure that he would not be able to tell anyhow! One afternoon I was busy at this task when a message was relayed to me in the basement that I was to hurry up and to put an extra cup on the tray as the chairman of the library committee had called in. I was in such a flurry I warmed the pot twice to make sure, but forgot to put any tea in it. As I was leaving his office, having put the tray on his desk, he turned to the chairman enquiring, 'and how do you like your tea, Mrs Townsend?'. 'Just as it comes, just as it comes', she replied graciously, and was rewarded with a cup of hot water! It was too much for me; I collapsed outside his office in a state of hysterical laughter. He was furious and later on I was subjected to half an hour's lecture and his conclusion that 'You, Miss Cox, may not feel that tea-making has anything to do with librarianship *but* if you fall down on a small job like this you will fail when it comes to greater things'. Had it not been for Miss Campbell's intervention I think he would have dismissed me on the spot. I suspect my crime was not so much omitting the tea in the pot as having the temerity to laugh about it; though heaven knows that laugh was involuntary and born of nerves.

He also, with the approval of the library committee, exercised his own censorship policy. All the books by such authors as Marie Stopes and Havelock Ellis and some of those by modern novelists such as Aldous Huxley and Ernest Hemingway were kept on a shelf outside his office which adjoined the children's library. Their titles appeared in the card catalogue in the main lending library with a note attached saying 'Any reader wishing to borrow this book should make application to one of the library assistants'. Then followed one of the most embarrassing procedures imaginable. Having been approached, in some bewilderment, by a borrower, the assistant would have to telephone Mr Skuce and, if he was in his office and not otherwise engaged, he would demand that the luckless individual be escorted to his office for a gruelling cross-examination as to why he, or she, wished to read this particular book. The young, the old, the curious and the bona fide scholar were all exposed to the same humiliating experience and, quite frequently, depending on the city librarian's assessment, were denied the book. Most public libraries at that time followed the practice of removing certain books from public view, presumably to protect 'minors', but I knew of no other library which carried out this personal 'vetting' process. What the borrowing public did not know, but what some of the library staff did, was that when members of the library committee and other senior members of the council requested 'weekend reading' from Mr Skuce, not only were they given the newest additions to the library book stock but were also offered any of the books on the shelf 'outside my office'.

Ruth Fasnacht in her book *The History of the City of Oxford* (Alden Press, 1954) pays warm tribute to the development of the public library services in Oxford during the first half of this century and says that this was largely due to the administration of Mr E.E. Skuce, who has earned 'the unanimous gratitude of the people of Oxford'. I would agree with her on the excellence of the service but in my opinion and certainly during my time there the credit for the administration of the book selection was in no small measure due to the deputy librarian, Margaret Campbell. A highly intelligent, cultured Scot, who did not suffer fools gladly, hers were the imaginative ideas that were put forward to the library committee and when the members agreed with

At Milham Ford School, Cowley Place in 1934. Joan Smart (now Merry) is on the left of the photograph

'Un trio sympathique' — Rose Nomdedeu, Monique Deporta, Olive Cox in the South of France, July 1935

My father and mother at Skinner's Bridge, Eynsham, late 1930s

them Mr Skuce took the credit; when they disagreed he blamed her. I had not only respect, but affection, for Peggy Campbell; most of the other girls regarded her as a hard task mistress but I found her very fair.

Except for Thursday, which was early-closing day, the libraries were open daily from 10 am until 7 pm and the staff worked very long hours for we had to be 'in' at 9.15 am and rarely left before 7.20 pm. We had a half day off on Thursdays and one 'early evening' at 5 pm or alternatively one 'shopping afternoon' from 3 pm until 5 pm. In addition at least two evenings a week were taken up with studying for our Library Association examinations which we did by correspondence courses. We learned to classify books according to the Dewey Decimal Classification Scheme and to catalogue them according to the rules of the British Museum but I never reached the dizzy heights of learning how to design libraries or how to budget for them. I began as a junior in the lending library, replacing returned books to their appropriate shelves, writing 'date labels' and 'cleaning books'. The last-named was a horrid job for we had to sponge dirty pages with a damp cloth and then buffer the filthy edges of the books with emery paper. Not a job for the fastidious for the dirt, dust and minute particles of paper from our vigorous rubbings settled in our eyes, our hair and our noses. When books became so dirty they did not respond to our efforts they were put to one side and eventually boxed up and sent to Oxford Prison with the exception of crime fiction which it was thought might bring new ideas to the prisoners! From time to time we removed an interesting collection of book-marks, banana skins, kipper bones and odd lists and notes. One such note read, 'Bert, If I perchance, my darling, should be out when you return the fish and the fried onions are in separate pans. Doris'.

The library had a large and widely differing readership, varying from the housewife who wanted a book 'with a bit of love in it' to university members searching for a volume which was not currently available in their college libraries. Oxford being Oxford the library numbered among its readers people who were already well-known, or who were to become 'household names', but, except for a few of them, my memories are vague. I clearly remember Denis Healey not only for his eyebrows which were black then and gave his face a brooding look but also because he invariably loped into the library at 6.45 pm and we were on tenter-hooks hoping he would have found his book by 7 pm which was closing time. During the war my great favourite was Lord Samuel who was always very apologetic that most of the books he required were in the basement. One Christmas he very diffidently, and with great delicacy, gave me a £5 note as a present. He explained that he had consulted his wife and she had said that with coupons, rationing and a general shortage of goods in the shops, this was quite the most sensible way of showing his appreciation. He need not have worried; I had never seen a £5 note before and I was speechless with pleasure and surprise for I would willingly have climbed the Himalayas for him if that is where the books he wanted had been housed! I was once sent to 'recover' an overdue book and collect the money due for fines from Leslie Banks the actor who was then living on Folly Bridge. The great man himself opened the door and patiently listened to my stumbling explanation for my visit. He apologised with enormous charm, invited me in for coffee while he looked for the book which he said one of his children had borrowed and before I left gave me his autograph. I was so dizzy with the excitement of it all I forgot to ask him for the 'fines' and I had to pay them myself when I got back to the library!

Mr Skuce's 'young ladies' were not without suitors, and flowers and poems were constantly being handed over with their 'returned' books by bashful or bumptious young men. The most flattering poem I received was written on blue paper in a flowering hand. It was addressed to 'The Girl in the Green Canoe'.

'A keen and eager eye revolves and roams
Along some bulging shelves of musty tomes,
An anxious glance is cast along the line
Of ranging books, for one I know is mine,
At last the sought-for prize is found
and with a smile of triumph turn around
To see a girl upon whose arm is raised
A towering pile of books, I gazed and gazed.
Deprived of speech, with madly beating heart
My tottering limbs would neither move nor start.
And then across my mind there draws a scene
of leafy boughs and grasses tall that lean
And sparkle in the mirrored summer rays
Of Cherwell's stream of green-decked banks and bays.
A green canoe along the course appears,
A slow and graceful pace it sets, and nears.
This self-same girl who's now before me stood
Was there, her hands upon a blade of wood.
She sits erect and straight with queenly grace
Her dipping paddle beats a rhythmic pace.
A scene like this was opened to my view;
I called her then the girl in the green canoe.
She really was a most enchanting creature,
Without delay I must away and greet her'.

But the poem was more romantic than the poet; he was short, thickset and pimply and I think he was called 'Truss'; so the poem was graciously acknowledged and any further overtures firmly rejected.

After a year or so, to my great delight, I was promoted to deputy to the children's librarian. I loved the children's library. It had light oak round tables and small chairs, and an enchanting frieze round the whole of the room depicting characters from *Alice in Wonderland*. Life moved at a much more leisurely pace than in the main lending library and the children were far less impatient than the adults. The children, too, came from very differing backgrounds; those from North Oxford were accompanied by a parent or a 'nanny' while those from St Thomas' and the Friars came in with their friends. I shall always remember two brothers from the Friars, who I always thought of as 'the Terrible Twins', for their surname was 'Bull' and they had been christened 'Horace' and 'Terence'. When asked their names they replied: 'Orry Bull and Terry Bull, Miss!'. These two lads who were voracious readers always brought brown paper covers to protect their books and, even if their wrists looked slightly murky, their hands were well-scrubbed for we attempted by various means to inculcate into our young readers a loving care of books. The book stock was excellent; since there was a strong demand for Angela Brazil, the Biggles books and Richmal Crompton's 'William' books these had to be in stock but we gave pride of place on the show cases to Arthur Ransome, Kenneth Grahame and Hugh Lofting as well as the more obvious classics. The non-fiction section was no less attractive. Helping young people to appreciate English literature was a very exhilarating and rewarding experience and is, I believe, one of the most important aspects of librarianship. Years later I was to disagree profoundly with those academics and intellectuals who wanted to charge public library readers for borrowing fiction while non-fiction could be borrowed free. I think the service should remain free, for recreational as well as education reasons. Who are we to deny the over-worked housewife or the factory worker the romantic novel or the detective story, and a few hours escape from drudgery into fantasy?.

When the children's librarian left to be married in 1939 I had hoped to replace her but at that time the library was developing its depot library and school library service and where, before, these had been part of the duties of several librarians it was decided to create a new post of librarian in charge of school and depot libraries. The new librarian would be entirely responsible for the book selection and the organising of voluntary helpers and would have to liaise with the Education Department (which paid half of the salary of this post) and headteachers. I accepted the challenge and never regretted it for, especially during the war, both of these services were of immense value to children, particularly evacuees, and adults living lonely and, because of limited transport, isolated lives on the outskirts of the City. There were four depot libraries, Wolvercote, Marston, Summertown and Donnington, in addition to two branch libraries, Temple Cowley and Bury Knowle at Headington. The branch libraries had the same opening hours as the St Aldates' libraries but the depots had one afternoon and one evening session a week. I would not like to calculate how many miles, so many of them in the 'black-out', I cycled during those years. At the schools, books were changed termly and heads and their staffs were encouraged to put forward lists of books and make other suggestions to improve the service. In this way I formed valuable relationships with teachers which stood me in very good stead when I later became a city councillor and a member of its education committee.

I did, however, have one very unpleasant experience which left me almost impotent with fury. One consignment of books I sent to a church school in Oxford was returned by the Head with a cryptic note saying he did not want any more library books for his school until the schools' librarian had learned not to send his pupils pornographic literature. Peggy Campbell and I puzzled over this comment and looked again and again at the volumes I had sent to find the offending book, or books, when we suddenly realised that the note had been slipped inside a book called *Great Masterpieces of the World* which contained reproductions of such famous paintings as Botticelli's *The Birth of Venus*. I went cold with shock and almost fainted at the thought that someone with such views was responsible for forming young minds. Seeing my distress, Peggy advised Mr Skuce, and he took her advice, not to challenge the decision but to react by not sending the school any more books. I am not sure that was a wise decision and years later when I was discussing this with a friend of mine who was the head of a large primary school I became convinced that we should, at least, have reported this incident to the Education Department. She said, 'Oh. I remember him; he was a very strange man. His wife was not allowed to enter any room he was in without first knocking. He had a nervous breakdown or something in the end'.

As I mentioned earlier I left the library service in 1944 and did not return to that, or any other, professional career. With the exception of Mr Skuce I liked all the staff I worked with and made friends with two of them who had also been at Milham Ford: Gladys Munday, who was four years older than me, and Peggy King who was a year younger. I never fully qualified as a Fellow of the Library Association and was content, mainly through indolence, to remain an Associate, but those were interesting happy years and there are still people around who remember me as 'Little Miss Cox in the Library'.

The long hours spent inside the library did not preclude an active social life outside its walls. My godmother had retired as Mother Superior of St Thomas' Convent and had gone to live in St John's Home on the Iffley Road where, I must shamefully admit, I very rarely visited her. I was, as my mother was always telling me, a great disappointment to Mother Anna Verena but I, for my part, found the rigidity of her views oppressive and her class-consciousness very disturbing. Unfortunately I have never learned the art of 'keeping a civil tongue in my head' and on occasions I disagreed with her in a far more forceful manner than she thought appropriate for a girl of my humble background. Relations between us became very strained and no one was more pleased than my father when my visits to her ceased entirely.

I did, however, return to regular worship at St Thomas' Church and, after the services in Nice Cathedral, I found High Mass on Sundays a fulfilling and satisfying experience. I became an occasional Sunday School teacher but, looking back, I am convinced we should have been better trained. I remember, at one class, telling the children the story of St Martin tearing his cloak in half and giving one half of it to a beggar. When in prim tones I pointed out that this was an excellent example of Christian charity and foolishly enquired how many of us would do the same I heard a small boy at the back remark, 'Well I wouldn't because our Mam would give me a good clip round the ear if I gave half my coat to a tramp'! I also joined the church dramatic society, St Thomas' Players, and acted in three memorable productions which, as the Church hall was in a state of such chronic disrepair, we performed at the Clarendon Press Institute in Walton Street. Flattering comments on my acting ability went straight to my head and, on occasions, I wistfully regretted that I had not had the opportunity of going on the stage. Perhaps, later on, this was the attraction of politics for me but I hope not! I was already, like a number of my generation, vaguely uneasy about the political situation.

Unemployment in Oxford was not the major problem it was in other parts of the country and my first knowledge of what being out of work could really mean came a few years earlier when I was on holiday in Portsmouth. I was going down to the beach with my mother and on the way we passed a long line of men who I thought were queuing for the cinema. I was struck by the expression of hopelessness on some of their faces and asked my mother why they looked so miserable because they waited to get into the 'pictures'. 'You silly girl', said my mother, 'they are not waiting for the pictures, they are waiting for their dole money'; she went on to explain what being on the dole meant. She finished by saying, 'And we should thank the good Lord that your father has a job because the money they get is hardly enough to keep body and soul together, poor things'. I was about eleven or twelve at the time and it made an indelible impression on me; so much so that when Ellen Wilkinson led the Hunger Marchers from Jarrow to London I could not contain my tears and was deeply disturbed by the suffering of the unemployed.

Abroad, Mussolini in Italy and Hitler in Germany were justifying their systematic destruction of human rights and the imposition of repressive regimes, where imprisonment and even death were meted out to anyone who opposed them, by asserting that this was the only way to save their respective countries from communism and anarchy. Mussolini was regarded in this country as a bit of a buffoon but I was terrified by the maniacal ravings of Hitler, which we heard over the radio, and more than a little disturbed by the growth of the British Union of Fascists led by Oswald Mosley. I had briefly encountered anti-semitism for the first time in France when Maman, referring with great contempt to a girl from the lycée who had been chosen to play at the conservatoire, spat out, 'Elle est juive'. I thought at first I had misheard or mistranslated Maman but sadly this was not the case. Naively I was unable to understand how people who professed to be Christian could be anti-Jew when Christ himself was a Jew. I had not yet learned that 'going to church' was not necessarily synonymous with Christianity. In spite of my uneasiness I did not come from a 'political' family and did not number among my friends anyone who was politically motivated, so I tended to keep my fears to myself. Looking back I think my attitude then was comparable to that of many young people today who have 'learned to live with the Bomb' and do not want their rosy cocoon of 'it will never happen' disturbed. That attitude was to change a few months later but meanwhile my social life continued although it was somewhat restricted by my father's extreme Victorian attitude. He insisted that, unless he gave me an occasional reprieve, I must be home by 9.30 pm and if I was going out with a boy he did not know, he would wait outside the theatre, cinema, or any other place of entertainment I was at, and follow a few paces behind us until we reached Old Christ Church Buildings. He would then go inside, wait a discreet five minutes and abruptly open the door and yell 'Olive, time you were in'. This was continued until he felt he could trust my companion. My boys laughingly still comment, 'Dad must have been head over heals in love with you Mum to put up with that'! I was not allowed under any circumstances to go out with undergraduates but this was not an uncommon restriction in respectable working-class families in St Thomas' as there had been several illegitimate births resulting from local girls' associations with students.

I was not allowed to use make-up, smoke or go into a pub; Syd got into terrible trouble one Christmas for taking me into a pub for a glass of sherry after delivering presents to relatives on Christmas Eve, and a pall hung over us for the whole of Christmas Day. My father expected me to dress in what he considered to be a decent and modest fashion. This required a hideous and useless garment called a liberty bodice; it was made of heavy cotton twill, was short sleeved and stretched from the neck to the thighs. It had two strips of buttons at the back and two at the front; each button being the size of a 5p piece. I never did discover what useful purpose, if any, those buttons served for they were certainly not ornamental and I dispensed with this wretched garment as often as I could. One night when I was going to a dance at the Carfax Assembly Rooms with other girls from the library, my father enquired, 'Have you got your liberty bodice on, Olive?'. I don't know why he bothered to ask for all those horrible buttons were showing through my dress as sixteen unsightly lumps. I went out of the house hotly rebellious at being subjected to these indignities and then suddenly stopped, returned to the house saying I had forgotten my handkerchief, slipped into my bedroom, took off the liberty bodice, and stuffed it under the mattress. Then I skipped off, with new heart, to the dance. My freedom was short-lived; I had only been there about half an hour when one of my library colleagues pointed out that my father was standing at the door with a brown paper parcel under his arm and a face like thunder. I made my miserable way towards the door and just before I got there my father unwrapped the parcel and took out my liberty bodice. 'Either you put this on or you come home', he roared. I went home.

Joan and I often met on Thursday afternoons as we both had a half-day then. While I had been in France her friendship with Arthur Witcomb had waned and finally ceased and she was now deeply in love with Denis Merry, who worked at the Bodleian and was studying for an Oxford University degree. Towards the end of July she suggested that when we next met it should be in the early evening and she would bring Denis and one of his friends along so that we could all spend the evening together. I suspected her of match-making and was a bit hesitant about the suggestion, asking her what form the evening would take. 'Well, if you would bring your canoe along (I had recently bought a large Canadian camping canoe from Gladys Munday at the library for the princely sum of £6) we could all go on the river together', she said. She was so eager I hadn't the heart to disappoint her and the date, the time and the venue were fixed. We were to meet at 6 pm on 5 August at the river's edge in Christ Church Meadows, I having previously cycled up to the boat-house at Iffley to fetch the canoe. It was to prove the most important date in my life for I met the boy who was not only to become my husband but also a companion and friend for the rest of my life and a profound influence on my political thinking.

The evening did not set off auspiciously. I was at the appointed place in good time, for my father had always impressed on me the importance of being punctual: 'Never be late, Olive, most of the things in life you borrow you can pay back but you can never pay back borrowed time'. They were at least ten minutes late and I sat there idly dipping my paddle in the water and getting more and more irritable. When they eventually arrived, Joan full of apologies for keeping me waiting, I regarded them with amazement and was overcome by an hysterical desire to giggle. Both the young men were dressed in white flannels and navy blue blazers looking for all the world as though they were about to take tea on a college barge and obviously having no idea how very wet one could get in a canoe! Introductions were effected; I had briefly met Denis once before but not, of course, his friend Edmund Gibbs, a shy, fair haired, blue-eyed young man nearing his eighteenth birthday. I was not prepared for what happened next for, as he shook my hand and murmured very properly 'How do you do', my heart turned a complete revolution as it had not done since the days of Nigel Gidney and I was lost. I can remember very little about the rest of the evening but when I returned home at 9.30 pm and my mother asked, 'What have you and Joan been doing?', I said, 'Mum, I have met the boy I am going to marry. He doesn't know and I don't think he even likes me but I am going to marry him however many boys I go out with before then'. 'Don't be so silly', my mother said, 'and don't repeat such rubbish to your father'. I heeded her advice about my father. I was not wrong in assessing Edmund's reaction to me: Denis confided to Joan who in turn told me, I am sure for my own good, that Edmund had said that he thought I was very pretty but a bit of a 'show-off'. However that did not deter him from accepting a suggestion from Denis that we all four should go to an early performance at the New Theatre (now the Apollo Theatre) the following Thursday. I accepted with alacrity and we agreed to meet at the corner of George Street and Victoria Court at 5.45 pm: so as to get a seat in the 'Gods' for sixpence but we should have to queue for at least half an hour. When I arrived Edmund was already there and told me, with some hesitation, that Joan and Denis would not be coming as Denis had been injured playing cricket that afternoon and Joan had been unable to contact me as we were not on the telephone at home. He enquired politely whether I still wanted to go the the theatre and I, with an almost complete disregard for the truth, replied, 'I have turned down another attractive invitation to come here so we might just as well'. Anxious to counteract his view that I was a 'show-off' we queued in comparative silence, our only conversation being confined to discussion of our mutual dislike of boiled marrow. I insisted on paying for my own ticket which I learned afterwards was a great relief to him as his pocket money was running out and Denis had promised to lend him a shilling. Nor did we talk much during the performance which, because it was 'out of term', was a variety show. We came out of the theatre just before 8.30 pm and because my father thought I was with Joan he was not, thank goodness, lurking outside in a shop door-way. We had to endure that later! I suspected he couldn't afford to take me out for coffee and I knew instinctively he would be very offended if I offered to pay for him, so there was no alternative but to walk home. We walked slowly down George Street until we reached Lower Fisher Row and then we leaned over the railings and gazed into the waters of the canal. I asked him whether he too was studying for a degree as he worked at the Bodleian with Denis and suddenly, as sometimes happens with shy reserved people, the flood gates opened and I became the confidant of all the things which had been disturbing him emotionally for the past two or three months.

Apparently he had been awarded a place at St Peter's Hall (now St Peter's College) and had intended taking it up the following October with a view to entering the Church after he obtained his degree. All this had changed dramatically for him when a few months earlier his much-loved sister, Paxina, had died at the age of fifteen years. He said that he no longer believed in God and could not go into the Church. To add to his unhappiness his mother, already grief stricken at the loss of her daughter, was desperately upset at his refusal to take up his place at St Peter's Hall and attempted to persuade him that his feeling about God was only temporary. When he stubbornly insisted that he knew he would not change his mind she became very angry and they were now scarcely on speaking terms. I could not think of any words to express my sympathy that would not sound trivial and wisely confined myself to asking him what he now intended doing. He told me that he had always been interested in accountancy and his father, an agnostic, who had been relieved, rather than upset, by his decision not to go into the Church had encouraged him to apply for a junior post in the treasurer's department of Oxfordshire County Council where he, like me, could attempt to gain a professional qualification by correspondence course. His application had been successful and he was going to County Hall at the beginning of September; meanwhile he had a temporary job at the Bodleian which was where he had met Denis. He seemed anxious to go on talking about religion but he was, I think, a bit shocked by my Anglo-Catholicism for his father, as well as being an agnostic, was almost virulently anti-Roman Catholic and was highly suspicious of the Oxford Movement. Although living in the parish of St Michael at the Northgate, Edmund and his mother had regularly attended St Peter le Bailey Church in New Inn Hall Street. The Gibbs family was friendly with the Chavasse family, which lived round the corner from them. The Rev C.M. Chavasse (later to become Bishop of Rochester) was the Vicar of St Peter le Bailey and also the Master of St Peter's Hall and this, no doubt, explains why the church was later incorporated into the college.

As we leaned over the railings talking I suddenly realised to my horror that 'Old Tom' of Christ Church had finished chiming its one hundred and one strokes some time before and I ought to have been safely indoors if I was not to invoke my father's wrath. Hurriedly explaining to a somewhat bewildered Edmund that my father was very strict about time I took to my heels and fled. Recovering from his surprise he pursued me and was just in time to see me turn into the passage-way of Old Christ Church Buildings. He told me afterwards that the Buildings, which he had never seen before, looked so much like a barracks he thought my father must be in the army! Having telephoned me next day at the library and been told that assistants were not allowed to take personal calls, he came into the lending library the following day ostensibly to change a book but really to ask me to meet him again. And thus began a love affair which has lasted over half a century. Looking back I suppose the secret of this lasting relationship has been the fact that we are opposites in temperament but alike in attitudes. Unlike me he is slow to anger and tolerant, and has the patience of Job which he has needed with me on occasions! We rarely disagree on political philosophy and on religion; although he professes to being an agnostic, his commitment to a Christian way of life and his acceptance of most of the teachings of Christ give me hope for his salvation. It was with some relief that I repeated to him a remark I had heard David Jenkins (the Bishop of Durham) make at a meeting I attended the other day that Christ came to save all mankind and not just those who go to church. When we first met he was almost painfully shy and I, to put it mildly, was something of an extrovert but, over the years, the gap has narrowed and we have both, I think, reached a middle ground.

It is not difficult to like Edmund and my father was no exception. The trial period with its attendant 'following behind ritual' was mercifully brief and I was commanded to invite him to Sunday tea. What I did not know then, but my father did, was that Edmund's father was a very popular left-wing councillor for the South Ward of Oxford. Although a very-well educated man with a Cambridge BA, a London BSc, and a Diploma in Education from Trinity College, Dublin, he championed causes of the poor and underprivileged in his own ward which included the Friars, and in the rest of Oxford. He later became known as the Baron of Cuttselowe for the leading role he played in the fight to demolish the infamous Cuttselowe Wall which divided a council housing estate from a private housing estate in Summertown. It was built across two main highways and he was not only concerned that it meant long extra journeys round the end of the wall for children to get to school and women to reach the shops, but that it represented an intolerable social distinction. Every effort, legal and illegal, to remove it failed, the owners of the private estate being able to prove in court, although Sir Stafford Cripps acted for the defence, that the roads across which the wall had been built belonged to them as they were part of the housing estate construction. Over twenty years later Edmund, then a councillor, and chairman of the city estates' committee, persuaded the council to purchase compulsorily the nine inch strip of land on which the wall stood and on a cold blustery morning in March 1959 he, himself, knocked out the first brick in the demolition process. It was a very emotional moment and turning to me he said, very quietly, 'At last I have been able to complete the task my father set out to do so many years ago'.

But my future father-in-law's political stance was not the only thing that appealed to my father. He had always hoped for a better life for me than had proved to be the lot of many of the girls in St Thomas' and the fact that the Gibbs family lived in a large house in St Michael's Street next to the Oxford Union and had a daily maid created a very favourable impression. To be fair to my father this would have been of no importance to him had Edmund not possessed the character and qualities he regarded as necessary in a companion for me. The invitation to tea provided him with an opportunity of assessing these. I dreaded this wretched tea; other people I had taken home were not important enough for me to worry about what they thought or what their reactions to my home and family would be but Edmund was desperately important. I worried about whether my father would be too abrasive, my mother too anxious to please and my surrounding so humble as to invoke a reaction of pity, my pride would not allow me to tolerate, in this boy I already loved so much. On the appointed Sunday Edmund met me from Sunday School and we slowly walked home, I wishing we could take steps backwards instead of forwards. But my fears were not realised. When we arrived at the door my mother was waiting there and as Edmund put out his hand to shake hers, which from force of habit she wiped on her pinafore before extending, that lovely sweet smile of hers lit up her whole face and he was immediately captivated. My father was so overcome at being addressed as 'Sir' that he behaved impeccably for the whole of the time Edmund was there. On later occasions Edmund was to disagree with my father profoundly and challenge him fiercely on his bullying attitude towards me but not on that Sunday evening. The tea would have put even the Gibsons' former feasts into the shade: not only was there a great variety of sandwiches, biscuits and cakes, but my mother's 'wedding china' had been brought out and the linen and lace tablecloth were whiter than driven snow. When it was time for Edmund to go I was so overcome with relief I almost wept.

I knew in advance that Edmund's mother was not kindly disposed towards me for she had confided to the mother of one of the girls who worked in the library with me that she thought I was too old for him (there was ten months difference in our ages) and that the differences in our backgrounds was too great. One evening when I was on counter duty in the lending library Sybil, whispering in my ear, pointed out a woman at the far end of the library and said, 'That's Edmund's mother. I have never seen her in here before so she is probably looking you over'. I was furious which was very unfair of me as my parents, in their own way, were just as anxious about the suitability of my friends. I was so angry that, fairly soon after this first distant encounter, when an invitation came for me to join the Gibbs' family for an 'after dinner' coffee I was minded to refuse. I regarded the invitation itself as a snub, for in St Thomas' our hospitality was such that we would not dream of offering anyone, except a casual visitor, just a drink. I had a lot to learn and a lot of deep-seated feelings of inferiority to lose!

I went because Edmund begged me to go, but with such feelings of antagonism on both sides it is not surprising that the evening was not an outstanding success. It was a strange occasion. We sat on chintz-covered chairs in their front drawing-room which was enormous by St Thomas' standards, drinking coffee out of delicate china cups. I found the company no less strange; Edmund's mother was young, fashionably dressed and wearing lots of jewellery. She was not a bit like my comfortable Mum nor for that matter had she the warm expansiveness of 'Maman'. Edmund's father, for his part, was much older than I had expected and, to my enormous surprise, wore a deer-stalker hat for the whole of the time I was there. When I asked about this afterwards Edmund explained that he very rarely took it off as he had a theory that he caught cold when he wasn't wearing it! However, even that was not so eccentric as the presence of another guest, who had been to dinner, a refugee Polish philosopher called Samuel Sopote who, I later learned, had written an obscure book called *The Theory of Sacrificial Obsession*. He had piercing blue eyes and a black bushy beard and was six feet tall and almost as wide. The tennis shoes he was wearing went very oddly with his black suit and every time he bowed, which he did frequently, even when he opened the door to let the family cocker spaniel, Judy, in, he bumped into a piece of furniture and more often than not sent books and ornaments flying. It was just as well that Edmund's younger sister Dulcina, who was then about seven or eight years old, was in bed for on later occasions I saw her reduced to helpless giggles as her mother, tight-lipped, gathered up pieces of broken china and glass after one of Professor Sopote's excesses. I was ill at ease under the family scrutiny and, as usual in such circumstances, behaved in a thoroughly unpleasant and brash way which only deepened my future mother-in-law's antipathy towards me. I think too that, very unfairly, she regarded me as responsible for Edmund's refusal to go into the Church although he had taken that decision months before I first met him. Edmund's father, although more tolerant in his reaction to me, tried to console her by saying that it was only calf love and Edmund would soon get over it but she was not to be comforted and for months afterwards invited a number of attractive and suitable young ladies, daughters of her friends, to the house in an effort to distract him. When this ploy failed she expressed concern for Edmund's future and never spoke to me more often than was necessary. This state of cold war between us continued for two or three years and must have been very distressing for Edmund. Eight years ago, when we celebrated our fortieth wedding anniversary with a splendid dinner which many well known city and county figures attended, I was amused when she said to me with a fond smile, 'Well you must admit, dear, they haven't been such bad years have they?'. I bit my tongue, laughed, kissed her on the cheek and replied, 'No, Ma, they have been rather better than you predicted'. Although Edmund's father was more kindly disposed towards me, and invariably courteous, I think he too believed Edmund could have made a better choice. In spite of his progressive and socialist views on most other

Edmund Gibbs and I (in the 'green canoe') in 1938

Our wedding at St Thomas' Church, 14 September 1940. My brother Syd is on the left

In September 1941

subjects, surprisingly he did not subscribe to the equality of the sexes. As far as he was concerned women were definitely the weaker sex and to be treated accordingly. We were not expected to advance a personal view on any serious subject and I think my tendency to do just that frequently irritated him. My mother-in-law, who was his second wife and twenty years his junior, deferred to him in everything and that was something I could not do, either for him, or any other man.

However, the relationship that really mattered was with Edmund and it opened up a completely different and exciting new world for me. I learned of the rights of the individual within a democracy and that conditions and events could be changed, even if slowly, by speech, by action and by the vote. It was no longer enough to sit back and feel sorry for the unemployed or vaguely uneasy about the growth of fascism abroad and in this country; it was a time for doing something about it. When Martin Luther King, in the early sixties, said, 'Evil is accomplished not only by the wicked who speak out but by the good who remain silent', I recognised it as a philosophy Edmund had instilled in me over a quarter of a century before. We were inseparable; the times we spent in our jobs or in studying for our professional examinations were only tedious periods to be endured until we could be together again. It would be pleasant to record that we never quarrelled but that would not be true as on occasions we fought fiercely and passionately, and not infrequently during one of these periods I would accept an invitation to go out with another boy but a letter or a telephone call would soon bring us running back together which is where we wanted, and needed, to be. Life was not, of course, all politics; we took picnics on the river in the famous green canoe and we went on long walks. Our favourite walk was through Old Marston and Elsfield, where we passed the Buchan family house, and on to Beckley for a lunch of bread, cheese, pickles and a glass of cider for sixpence. Occasionally we went to dances or to the theatre but not often as our finances had to be carefully managed! It ought to have been a time of unimaginable joy yet all these memories are overshadowed by the remembrance of the overriding fear, constantly with us then, of an impending second world war.

7 · SPAIN AND MUNICH

In the nineteen thirties St Giles was to Oxford what Trafalgar Square and Hyde Park are to London and the nation today. Almost all protest meetings, demonstrations and marches either began or ended there. There were, of course, far fewer cars about, and the Martyrs' Memorial, the War Memorial and the wide tree-lined spaces, now filled with parked cars, between the pavement and main thoroughfare on both sides of St Giles, made splendid focal points for dissent.

On most Sunday evenings Edmund and I were irresistibly drawn to St Giles to open-air meetings organised by the Communist Party and addressed by Abe Lazarus, often known as Firestone Bill because of a successful strike he had organised in the Firestone Rubber Company. In all my years in political life I have never met anyone with a more magnetic personality than Abe. Of medium height, with flaming red hair and startlingly blue eyes, his ringing voice could be heard, without the aid of a microphone, from one end of St Giles to the other. It is said that the dons in St John's used to tremble over their port as he prophesied a workers' revolution in this country! Like Aneurin Bevan, at a later period, he had the gift of reducing people to tears at one moment and delighted laughter the next, but for me Abe's voice always rang truer than Nye's. When he talked of the starving people of Europe he could divorce me from most of my week's pocket money with one sentence although I knew, in advance, I would incur my father's wrath on returning home.

Crowded public meetings both pro and anti-fascist were also held in Oxford's Town Hall in the late thirties and I remember two in particular. One, where the platform shared by Professor Haldane, G.D.H. Cole, Victor Gollancz and Edmund's father was invaded by violent young fascists, and the meeting broken up by them. Another, addressed by Sir Oswald Mosley, where anyone in the audience daring to venture a contrary point of view was summarily and with unbelievable brutality ejected. Both Frank Pakenham (now Lord Longford) and Dick Crossman were thrown down the Town Hall stairs that night and suffered broken limbs. It was said, although I did not witness it, that the police 'looked the other way'.

Edmund and I were not members of the Communist Party but nor were we, for that matter, members of the Labour Party. Edmund's father had been elected to the city council in 1934 as a Ratepayers' candidate, the Ratepayers' Association then being on the left of politics rather than to the right as it is today, but he joined the Labour Party in 1936 or 1937 and became a member of a Labour Group which included Frank Pakenham (a councillor for the Cowley and Iffley Ward) and Dick Crossman who represented Headington and Marston. He was later to oppose, bitterly, Frank Pakenham's nomination as a Parliamentary candidate because of Frank's conversion to Roman Catholicism.

But political lines were far less sharply drawn then than they were to become when the Cold War started. The growing menace of fascism abroad and at home tended to bring together, in a common cause, all those of us who were left of centre and the Civil War in Spain acted as a catalyst. When General Franco in 1936 launched an attack to overthrow the liberal Republican Government in Spain and establish a military dictatorship, Germany and Italy broke a non-intervention pact and sent arms and troops in support of Franco. The USSR followed suit, supplying arms to the Republican Government forces. In this country Chamberlain's Conservative Government was determined to use the non-intervention pact as an excuse for doing nothing although Franco with the help of Germany and Italy was inflicting terrible defeats on the beleaguered Republicans, which eventually led, in 1939, to the establishment of a fascist state ruled by Franco and which Spain had to endure for almost forty years. There was a groundswell of feeling in this country, from people of all political parties, but mainly from those 'left of centre', that the British Government was wrong, that the non-intervention pact had already been broken and the Spanish Government, democratically elected in 1931, was being attacked by minority forces in Spain, aided and abetted by two foreign fascist powers. The suspicion also lurked in some of our minds that Chamberlain was not in any way anxious to oppose Hitler. Tremendous demonstrations were mounted all over England, and Oxford was no exception. We marched from the Plain to St Giles carrying political and Trades Union banners and chanting 'Arms for Spain' and 'Down with Chamberlain'. Marching next to me was the young man, with beetling eyebrows, who made such good use of the city library, Denis Healey!

Chamberlain, unmoved by these protests, continued his non-intervention policy and many young men in this country joined the International Brigade to give support and, in many cases, their lives, for the defence of democracy in Spain. One of these was Jack Jones, later to become one of the most distinguished Trade Union leaders of this century whom I am proud to number among my friends. When in September 1937 I paid by promised visit to France to visit Maman, Papa and Monique, I came back on a Cross Channel Ferry from Dieppe to Newhaven with young men, some of them wounded, who had fought with the International Brigade. Their stories of the devastation in Spain and the merciless bombing of towns, particularly in the Basque country, made me sick and faint but reinforced my passionate belief that the British Government was wrong to stand aside from this conflict. However Chamberlain persuaded the majority of people that this was none of our business; it was a trial of strength between two opposing ideologies, fascism and communism. And thus the scene was set for World War Two.

In the nineteen sixties I was to protest vigorously about the war in Vietnam and, looking back, it is sad to contemplate how similar were the attitudes of the British public to both the Spanish and the Vietnam wars. People's imagination was fired, and their hearts touched by the victims, especially the children, of the bombings in Spain and never more so than after the destruction of Guernica. At a Ball held at the Town Hall at the beginning of 1938 hundreds of pounds were raised for the Spanish Relief Fund. Similarly, during the war in Vietnam, money poured in to help the Vietnamese people irrespective of which side they were on. Yet in both cases the majority were not prepared to examine in any depth the political implications of these wars. There is in Britain a near pathological fear of communism which forces people to close their eyes to the right of other people to choose their own form of government. I value democracy above most other things but I do not subscribe to the view, commonly held and glibly voiced, that the only freedom is the freedom of speech and action. In the poorer countries of this world, and two thirds of the world's population is hungry to the point of starvation, the freedom to eat and survive is a far more basic freedom.

While the Civil War was raging in Spain, Hitler was also relentlessly pursuing his territorial ambitions in other parts of Europe nearer to Germany. With the assassination of Austria's Chancellor Dolfuss in 1934, and the coup by Austrian Nazis in 1936, his occupation of that country in March 1938 seemed, for most of us, inevitable. But it came as an unpleasant shock to many people in Britain, who preferred to close their ears to Hitler's maniacal ravings rather than recognise the threat that he posed. Yet even Chamberlain's Government began to have serious misgivings as he turned his attention to Czechoslovakia and claimed that in part of it, the Sudetenland, the population was mainly German. Fears reached fever pitch by the beginning of September after the Government issued thirty-eight million gas masks and ordered air raid trenches to be dug in the London parks. At the end of September Chamberlain, in desperation, flew to Munich for a meeting with Hitler at which he hoped to resolve the Czech crisis. He returned to England on 30 September holding an umbrella in one hand and a piece of paper in the other. He waved the paper aloft, to waiting reporters and photographers, and proclaimed triumphantly 'Peace in our time'. The 'peace' was at the cost of the dismemberment of Czechoslovakia and the transfer to Hitler and his Nazis of the Sudetenland. It was said that for many months afterwards no one smoking a pipe dared appear on the streets of Czechoslovakia in case he was taken for an Englishman. 'Our time' lasted less than a year. I think it is true to say though, that Chamberlain's action commanded majority support in England, and most people were overjoyed that an immediate war had been averted, but for Edmund and me, and many like us, this was a further shocking example of British appeasement; nothing would now stem Hitler's ambitions.

That same evening Edmund went off to St Cross School in Holywell and joined a newly formed Territorial Unit, the 252nd Anti-Aircraft Battery. I put a brave face on his decision but cried myself to sleep that night. Anyone less like a military type than Edmund it was difficult to imagine, and I was worried and frightened for him, and for our future together, but I knew that, holding the views he did, he had no alternative. The next day I joined the Town Hall's Air Raids' Precaution Group.

In the latter part of October, Oxford City was provided with an opportunity of passing its verdict on Chamberlain's 'sell out' of Czechoslovakia in exchange for his 'Peace in our time'. The Conservative Member of Parliament, Captain R.C. Bourne (the object of our childhood ridicule), had died, and a by-election had been declared. There were three candidates for the seat: the Hon Quintin Hogg, son of Lord Hailsham, who was a lawyer and Fellow of All Souls, for the Conservatives; Patrick Gordon Walker, an Oxford academic with pronounced anti-communist views for Labour, and for the Liberals an attractive twenty-three year old Welshman, Ivor Davies, who had recently graduated from Edinburgh University (Ivor, together with his wife Jean later became close personal friends of Edmund and me). Quintin Hogg was a Chamberlain supporter, and right from the start of the campaign it was obvious that this was to be no ordinary election; it would be fought on the issue of foreign policy and not on the usual familiar platform of home affairs. It would be the first public testing of appeasement and the result would be of enormous interest, not least to Hitler, Mussolini, and Roosevelt. Ivor Davies, quickly sensing this, and realising that a Conservative majority of 6000 votes would be difficult to shake, decided that drastic action was needed. With a political and personal integrity which characterised the whole of the rest of his public life, he suggested that the Labour and Liberal candidates should withdraw in favour of an agreed 'Independent' candidate.

The choice was Dr A.D. Lindsay, the Master of Balliol and a former Vice-Chancellor of Oxford University. Patrick Gordon Walker was reluctant to withdraw his candidature but was finally persuaded to put the matter before the Oxford City Labour Party for decision. Edmund and I, not being members of the Labour Party, were not present at the special meeting called to discuss the issue but, judging by reports from Edmund's father and others, it was conducted in an atmosphere of extreme bitterness; only by a very narrow majority was the proposal that Gordon Walker should withdraw in favour of Dr Lindsay carried. Certainly, many years later, when canvassing for my own Council seat, I discovered voters who resigned from the Labour Party that night and never rejoined it. The Labour Party philosophy at that time appears to have been on very similar lines to that which governed their attitude towards 'tactical voting' in the 1987 General Election. When Dr Lindsay's candidature was finally declared there were only ten days to go to polling day and it was generally believed that Frank Pakenham paid the 'lost' deposits of the former Labour and Liberal candidates.

It was a strange election and I have never worked in any other election like it. Helpers from all political parties flocked into Lindsay's camp but they were mainly from the University. The 'town' itself appeared to stand aside from what they probably regarded as 'gown infighting'. My father, curiously, was an exception; he was so impressed when Dr Lindsay canvassed him that he put a poster and his photograph [of Lindsay] in our window. Nor was there any official help from the Labour Party which I suppose was anxious to avoid any further resignations of its members. Fierce arguments raged among my library colleagues; most of them came from comfortable conformist Conservative backgrounds and were supporters of Hogg, but there were two exceptions. One of these was my friend Gladys Munday. Her parents were strong Labour supporters, but Gladys had fallen in love with a German law student, Fritz Fischer, who had been studying in Oxford in the summer of 1937. Fritz, courageously, was not a member of the Nazi Party and held left wing views (after the war he became a councillor in Heidelberg representing the Social Democratic Party) and Gladys, who worried for his safety, was unusually silent during the election. The other was Peggy King, whose father played in the orchestra at the New Theatre. She held conservative views but was won over by my burning enthusiasm and a couple of Knickerbocker Glorys at Lyons Corner House at Carfax. I don't know whether the tenpence each I paid for those delicious ice-cream confections amounted to bribery but it was money well spent!

For ten glorious days we became fanatical followers of Lindsay; we addressed leaflets, we canvassed, and we carried banners shouting 'Hitler wants Hogg, Hitler wants Hogg, A vote for Hogg is a vote for Hitler' and, I am ashamed to say, in moments of extreme youthful vulgarity, 'Squinting Pig'. Edmund occasionally joined us but I think he found our exuberance a bit overwhelming and was happier in the more sober company of his father whom he accompanied to political meetings. I have serious doubts as to whether our canvassing was of any value to the campaign at all because unless the door was actually slammed in our faces we believed every voter was pro Lindsay. Such was our conviction that when the poll closed on that eventful October day we were convinced that the result was a foregone conclusion and that Dr Lindsay was Oxford's new Member of Parliament. Edmund, Peggy and I stood in St Aldates outside the building which is now the gas showrooms, waiting to hear the result officially declared so that we could cheer our heads off and boo our opponents. After what seemed an unconscionable time a door opened and the mayor, the town clerk, the two candidates and their wives, appeared on the stone balcony above the main town hall entrance. Their expressions should have been a warning to me, as the Tory mayor was smiling, Quintin Hogg was beaming and Dr Lindsay was expressionless, but I was not then as well versed in elections as I am now. The result was solemnly proclaimed and I stood in stunned disbelief, with tears pouring down my face, as Quintin Hogg was declared the duly elected member of Parliament for the Oxford Constituency. In vain did Edmund attempt to comfort me by pointing out that the Tory majority had been cut by half, because for me there was only a winner and a loser and Dr Lindsay had lost.

Around 1937 Edmund's father, who had been worried about the lack of recreational and leisure facilities for the young and the old in his ward, persuaded the city council to allow a no longer used pumping station in Lake Street, off the Abingdon Road, to be converted into a centre for such activities. He enlisted help from the clergy, school masters, political parties, Trade Unionists and local tradesmen in the mammoth task of turning this unlikely building into what was to become the forerunner of a community centre. He set up a committee and, fired by his enthusiasm, the conversion except for the laying of public services, which the city council paid for, was achieved by voluntary labour.

There were facilities for indoor games such as darts and table tennis, a sewing room for dressmaking and other needlework, and a large hall which could be used for social events or as a gymnasium. An all party committee, of which Mr Gibbs was the chairman, was set up to run what had now become known as the South Ward Social Guild and which is still in use today as the South Oxford Community Centre. People paid a small membership fee, and additional finance was obtained by letting out the main hall for dances, wedding receptions and public meetings. A licence was successfully applied for, and a bar opened which contributed largely to the running costs. The Guild was run entirely voluntarily, and catered for the needs of the whole of the South Ward from the Friars to the Weirs Lane housing estate. It attracted only a small grant from the city council. My future mother-in-law was a member of the committee and her attitude towards me was considerably softened by the time and energy I put in to building up a small library there and to helping with children's parties and other events.

As I mentioned earlier, in the late summer of 1937, I paid my promised visit to my 'French family' and spent a week with them in Juan-les-Pins and a week in Nice. Again it was for me a time of mixed emotions. The prospect of a fortnight away from Edmund seemed like an eternity but the warmth of their welcome was very moving. Monique was now sixteen years old, unusually tall, and lovelier than ever. She was still at the Lycée but unable to make up her mind whether to follow English or Music as a career. My French, which I had neglected when I returned home, came back in a flash and we enjoyed all the old jokes, sang all the old songs and revisited familiar and much-loved haunts. Maman complimented me on my wardrobe and said she was delighted to see I had developed a good dress sense. I realised again just how much I loved them all and how much they had done for this former 'petit de loups'. When the time came to say goodbye at Nice station Monique was there and I made tearful promises to come back again in two years' time. Thank God I did not know that I would never see them again.

Edmund met me at Victoria and vowed that we would never be parted again for such a length of time. I teasingly asked him what he thought we should do about future holidays as I was sure it would be easier to spend them at home than to persuade my father to allow us to go away together! To my astonishment he replied, '*That* is something I have given a great deal of thought to'. From subsequent conversations it was quite obvious that he had done just that and in his usual very thorough way. We were to go to Paris for ten days in the following June! As we both held very junior local government positions, and those in senior positions always chose their holiday dates first, June and September were the most likely months to be left for us, and since Edmund wanted to share France with me he thought Paris would be the ideal place for that time of year. Having decided that, he now sought my help in finding a family (had the Deportas any relatives or friends there?) or a boarding house where we could stay. I mentioned this to Peggy Campbell, the deputy librarian, and she immediately offered to write to some friends of hers, Monsieur and Madame Colbert, who ran a small 'pension' in the Rue de Faubourg St Honoré just off the Champs-Elysées. Miraculously they could take us and on terms we could afford. We now had the greatest hurdle to overcome – my father's permission – but, with an unexpectedness he occasionally displayed, he raised no objection at all. He was a great admirer of Miss Campbell, whose directness of approach appealed to him, and if she had recommended where we were to stay who was he to disagree?. However, with the disappearance of one hurdle another appeared. Edmund's mother was horrified: 'Go to Paris on your own?, What *would* people think? Never would she agree to such a thing'. Edmund's father felt bound to come to her support – he may even have agreed with her – and our dream collapsed.

The situation was rescued by my father who, I sometimes think, would have made a far more effective politician than I have ever been! On learning the reason for my tears he said nothing, but put his hat and coat on, and made his way to St Michael's Street intent on confronting Edmund's mother. I wasn't there of course – he had left me at home – but the story slowly emerged. Mrs Gibbs answered his ring at the door and invited him in saying, 'Is anything wrong Mr Cox?'. 'Nothing at all', replied my Dad, 'I wanted to thank you for your concern about my daughter'. Before the astonished woman could reply he went on remorselessly, 'When our Olive told us she and Edmund were going to France together her mother and I were very relieved because we have always been worried about her travelling alone on the Continent and we were glad that Edmund would be going with her this time to look after her. Thank goodness we have learned in time that you do not trust him to take good care of her. Her Mum and me are very grateful to you'. Poor Mrs Gibbs, faced with a situation where it could be thought that her son was not good enough for me instead of the other way round, she collapsed immediately, and said it had all been a great mistake: we had misunderstood what she had said.

So we had our holiday in Paris and it was pure magic. The sun shone gently and Monsieur and Madame Colbert treated us as they would their own family and often accompanied us on our expeditions. We packed so much into those ten days: the Eiffel Tower, the Sacré Coeur, the Left Bank, the Louvre, the Musée de Cluny, the Bois de Boulogne, Versailles and the Trianon, and the never-ending delight for me of window-shopping in the Champs-Elysées and the Rue de Faubourg St Honoré itself. We did not go to the Moulin Rouge or the Folies Bérgère. The last two were not really 'our scene' and in any case we were too exhausted in the evenings after dinner to do anything but chat amiably to the Colberts and play the occasional game of cards. I shall always be grateful to my father for making it possible for it was the only holiday we were to have together, and on our own, for almost thirty years.

In February 1939 I celebrated my twenty-first birthday. Among many other presents, my father gave me twenty-one pounds, my mother twenty-one shillings, and Edmund a silver pencil. We had a party at the South Ward Social Guild to which both families came, together with Joan and Denis, Peggy and Gladys and a few old friends from St Thomas', including Edna and Cyril Ashmall, at whose wedding a few years previously I had been a bridesmaid. Later that evening my happiness was considerably dimmed when Gladys took me to one side and told me that she intended going to Germany in May to marry Fritz. 'Oh *no*!', I said, 'You must not go – there is going to be a war'. 'I know', she replied, 'Fritz had warned me but I thought you would realise that it is *because* of a war and not *in spite* of it that I want to go. I cannot bear to be parted from Fritz for the duration of a war'. She went on to say that she had not yet broken the news to her mother and father but would have to do so within the next week. My heart was ready to break for them; she was an only child and her mother was a pacifist. I wept but she put her arm round me and said, 'Come on Olive, cheer up, I don't want to spoil your party. I did not mean to tell you tonight but seeing you and Edmund together I acted on impulse because I thought you would understand. Will you please promise to visit my parents regularly when I have gone? It would be such a relief for me if you could, because they are both very fond of you; mother particularly so'. The promise was given and kept. How could anyone do otherwise?

8 · WAR

There was now, I think, very little doubt in the minds of the majority of people that a war with Germany was inevitable; the only question remaining was 'when' and events moved very rapidly in 1939 confirming most people's fears that we should not see the year out in peace. In March Hitler, already having been given Sudetenland on a plate, made the excuse that there was a political unrest in Czechslovakia, marched on Prague and annexed the whole of the Republic. In the tense atmosphere of this further invasion, rumours were rife that his next objective was Poland. This goaded Chamberlain at the end of the month into giving a personal guarantee that Britain would defend Poland's independence should it be threatened. In consequence he expanded the Territorial Army and introduced the Military Training Act which was a limited form of conscription. In spite of this, people carried on with their daily lives, making plans for the future, and Edmund and I were no exception. We decided that we would like to go to Paris again, stay with the Colberts, and visit the places we had not time to see before. September was the month we chose as Edmund would be spending the whole of August at a Territorial camp in Cornwall, and I felt I would like to spend the long four week period without him in visiting Gladys in Germany. She was now married and living in Dresden and repeatedly wrote inviting me to stay with her and Fritz. It was finally arranged that I would spend ten days with them at the end of August and then join Edmund in Paris.

But the political position deteriorated rapidly in the summer of 1939. To the horror and consternation of most people, and particularly of those of us on the left of British politics, the Russo-German pact was signed in August 1939. It felt like the end of the world to me and certainly the end of everything I believed about the political integrity of Communist Russia. How *could* they ally themselves with the infamy of fascism? Three days after the announcement of this pact the British Government signed Chamberlain's personal guarantee to Poland.

Notwithstanding all these sinister happenings, and partly, I suppose, because as far as an outright war was concerned 'wolf' had been cried so often, I determinedly went ahead with my plans to go to Dresden. Fritz, with his usual courage, had written to me at the beginning of August warning me against coming, but this, together with my father's raging, and Mr Gibbs' reasoned arguments, only stiffened my resolve to go. I became very stubborn and unreasonable about the whole project. When threats were made to steal my passport I immediately transferred it from my drawer to my handbag, carrying it with me everywhere and sleeping with it under my pillow. I bought my ticket. Looking back I think I was as frightened as anyone but my obstinacy was governed by two contradictory factors. In cancelling my holiday I would be admitting to myself the inevitability of an imminent and terrible war but, paradoxically, I wanted to see Gladys again before it happened. As is usual with me, where threats and condemnations failed to change my mind, loving persuasion did. Edmund wrote to me from his camp in Bude gently telling me that if war broke out while I was in Dresden I could be interned and that I might be there for some months or even for the duration of the war. He told me that this would come near to breaking his heart; he was so worried he could not sleep at nights and although he understood my feelings he hoped I would not go. He begged me to go to the travel company and cancel my ticket but, at the same time, urged me to buy a ticket from Oxford to Paris so that when he finished his camp at the end of August we could still go to France. I think he knew the latter would never happen but he wanted to give me something to look forward to. I did as he asked me. Having taken this decision Mrs Gibbs suggested that I take a week's holiday with her and Dulcina on the Isle of Wight. Mr Gibbs' health was failing and she needed a rest. I was glad of the thought of something to do and on Saturday 26 August we left Oxford for Sandown. The weather was good and, although the boarding house we booked at the last moment was appalling, I was happy enough counting the days until I would see Edmund on the following Saturday before setting off to Paris with him the next day. The sun shone and people enjoyed themselves in a kind of frenzied activity but in Europe the black clouds had massed and the storm was about to break. The papers, and the radio, daily carried warnings that Hitler was about to invade Poland, and Britain had guaranteed its independence. Visitors began returning to the mainland in droves and I told Mrs Gibbs on the Thursday that I thought we, too, should return home. She made a mild protest that we had paid our accommodation up until the Saturday but when I told her that if we left it until then we might be stranded on the Island for some days, or even weeks (which proved to be the case for some holiday-makers), she agreed. We left for home on 1 September, the day Hitler invaded Poland, and the journey back to Oxford was an absolute nightmare.

I don't know what, if any, were the regulations governing the number of passengers on the boat ferry but it was perfectly obvious that there were far too many people on our boat and at one point I thought it was going to sink. The trains were so packed that no one could pass along the corridors; not that it would have been of any use if they could, because the lavatories had at least four people crushed into them. Having left Sandown at 10 am we eventually chugged into Oxford at 4 pm and the first person I saw on the platform was Syd who was attempting to cover any 'war stories' although we were not yet officially at war. He told me that it was strongly rumoured that the 252nd Battery had gone straight from Bude to Gibraltar. The miseries and uncertainties of war were never more starkly revealed to me than they were at that moment; I could not believe I might not see Edmund for months, or perhaps years, and I hadn't even had the chance to say 'Goodbye' to him. There was no news of him at his home or at mine and I was in agony of misery wondering what had happened to him and where he was. Desperate for something to do, to occupy my mind, I called in at the ARP office in the Town Hall and was immediately sent off to St Mary and St John School in East Oxford where evacuee children from London were being assembled before being taken to various families which had offered to 'foster' them in the event of war. The school hall presented a heartbreaking sight: it was packed with children of all ages and sizes. Some were well-dressed and well-nourished, others were skinny, pasty-faced and shabbily dressed, but all of them had one thing in common: identity labels securely attached to them and their luggage. They all looked frightened and 'lost' and many of them were crying. It was not a happy experience attempting to get all those children accommodated. I know that some attempt had been made in advance of their arrival to 'match' children with families but it was an almost impossible task and it was obvious that many families, some of them 'respectable working-class households', were very shocked at the appearance and condition of the poor frightened mites standing on their doorsteps waiting to be taken in. However, very few of these children were actually 'refused'; those that were, were eventually taken in elsewhere, but the initial rejection must have been a heart-rending experience for them.

I worked feverishly over the whole weekend but on the Saturday evening a great weight was lifted from me when I called in at Edmund's home and his mother said he had telephoned to say that he was stationed at Clapham Common on a gun-site there. He could not say more but I later learned that the battery had got as far as Waterloo Station but was then diverted to Clapham. War was officially declared on the Sunday morning but it came as no shock for unofficially we had been at war since the previous Friday when Hitler invaded Poland. I worked until late on the Sunday night at the evacuee centre at St Mary and St John School until the last child had been taken care of. I then cycled down to the boat-house at Iffley Fields and slowly paddled my canoe up the Thames and the Cherwell. The City was in complete darkness for the ARP wardens were already patrolling the streets to see that the black-out regulations were enforced. As I quietly made my way upstream the darkness was pierced by searchlights from various RAF stations which made patterns of light on the dark waters and I was gripped by a terrible loneliness and fear. When would this nightmare end?

Perhaps it is just as well that we did not know the war was to last for over five and a half years and, in my case, that Edmund would not be 'demobbed' until a year later than that. Too many books have been written, and too many films made, for me, even if I were capable of writing it, to attempt a potted history of 1939 to 1945. Today's generation is well aware of the appalling loss of life and the terrible bombing and destruction of our major cities. What they may not be aware of is the minor tragedies of the war: the years of our youth so cruelly snatched from us and which we could never recapture. I am bitterly resentful that Edmund and I never had an opportunity of enjoying the early years of married life; by the time he came home our son Andrew was almost two years old and they were relative strangers to one another. How much more fortunate was our second son, Simon, who was born after the war, and had the benefit of his father's company from birth.

Looking at other people's tragedies one can only be thankful that 'our war' was a relatively safe one. Except for a stray bomb jettisoned into an allotment by a returning German plane, Oxford was never bombed. At the time of the Baedeker raids we expected to be a prime target and when we weren't it was whispered among the townspeople that it was because the University laboratories were full of German spies! Although several of my childhood and teenage friends were killed, mostly in the air but some at sea or in the Middle or Far East, no one in the Cox family was killed. Edmund spent the whole of the war years on gun-sites in this country, only going to Europe at the end of the war to investigate Italian financial assets. Syd who joined the navy was stationed first at Fareham and then in Belgium. The horror of it all was that one was never free of anxiety and fear; no sooner did I receive news from Edmund that he was safe after the BBC had announced that there had been a raid on that part of the country where he was stationed, than another raid had taken place.

Poor Joan had a much worse war. She and Denis were married in November 1939, and in January Denis was part of the British Expeditionary Force which went to France and Belgium. He was due for leave in May 1940 but he was captured at Dunkirk as he boarded the boat for home. He was officially posted as 'missing' and Joan had to wait four agonising months before she knew what had happened to him. The 'good news' that he was a prisoner of war in Germany she received on the day I was married. Dear Joan, although I had been a bridesmaid at her wedding, in view of her anxiety about Denis, she preferred not to be a matron of honour at mine but no one could have been more helpful than she was in the weeks preceding my marriage. We wept together, before I went to church, as we lovingly pored over her telegram from the War Office.

For a marriage that has lasted forty-eight years it had a most unpropitious start. On 9 September, six days after war was declared, I received a pre-paid telegram from Edmund with the cryptic message, 'Will you be engaged'. Equally brief and to the point I replied, 'Yes'. I knew that on his Gunner's pay (he did not apply for a commission until 1942) he would not be able to afford an engagement ring and, feeling slightly self-conscious, I went off to a jewellers called Ballard's at the corner of Carfax and Queen Street and bought my own. It was a small solitaire diamond, set in 22 carat gold, and cost me £7. For weeks afterwards I never lost an opportunity of placing my left hand where the light would catch it and send flashes of fire from my diamond! We decided, much to my father's displeasure, that we would, if Edmund was still in this country, be married the following September. Poor Dad, who expected our engagement to follow the pattern of most working-class engagements and be of several years duration, was furious, and when first hearing the news shouted, 'You haven't enough money to be buried on, let alone married'. When I replied that we were preparing for marriage, and not death, he slammed out of the house in a fury and my mother said to me reproachfully, 'I do wish you wouldn't go round looking for ways to upset your father'! Since I was over twenty-one years of age there was very little he could do about it and slowly he became reconciled to the idea.

After the fall of France in 1940 it was a relatively quiet summer and, although rumours were rife that Hitler was about to invade Britain, Edmund and I went ahead with our plans and set the date of our wedding for 19 September (the date still engraved in my wedding ring) as he was entitled to a week's leave and we could spend four days honeymoon in Torquay. Preparations were necessarily rushed as we did not know the date of his 'leave' with any certainty until a few weeks beforehand, a difficulty experienced by everyone else during the war. On the evening of 12 September, to my horror and consternation, Edmund telephoned me at the library to tell me that all normal leave had been cancelled but, in the special circumstances of our wedding, his Commanding Officer had granted him thirty-six hours 'compassionate' leave which was to start at 8 am on Saturday 14 September and if we wanted to be married it would have to be on that day. Edmund did not tell me the reasons but I learned later that news had reached the High Command that Hitler was about to launch an all out air offensive that weekend. I was horrified but there was no alternative to accepting the Commanding Officer's offer other than postponing our wedding indefinitely. And so we became married on the day that afterwards became known as 'Battle of Britain Day'. All was feverish activity after Edmund's call. I telephoned Father Jalland at St Thomas' Church who accepted the change of date calmly; I rushed off to the dress-maker who, with less calm, bewailed the fact that she had only one sleeve in my wedding dress, but said that she would see what she could do. Edmund's aunt, recently evacuated from London, who begged and borrowed scarce ingredients to make a wedding cake, burst into tears and said, 'The icing will never have time to dry'. But the real problem was Mr Skuce, the city librarian, who said that Saturday was a very busy day at the library and he had no time in which to find a replacement for me. It did cross my mind that Edmund would have even more difficulty finding a replacement but I held my rebellious tongue and eventually reached a compromise whereby I agreed to work on Saturday morning until 12.30 pm, although the marriage ceremony was to be at 2.15 pm. Joan and Syd between them went round informing guests of the change of date and doing a hundred and one tasks connected with this wretched change of plans.

I woke to a light early Autumn mist, but the promise of a beautiful day, on the Saturday morning, and cycled off to St Thomas' Church to take Communion at 8 o'clock before going to the library at 9 am. My library colleagues were very disappointed that they had been denied the chance of attending the wedding which they were going to do had it been on the Thursday which was 'early closing day'. I was rushed off my feet for the whole of the morning, but at 12.30 pm promptly I cycled furiously home and in the limited time available got dressed, adjusted my veil, and inspected my two bridesmaids Dulcina and her friend, Tessa Halliday, whose parents were regular worshippers at St Thomas' Church. I wore a very plain ivory silk dress with a high neckline and a short veil secured with a circlet of camellias. I carried a bouquet of crimson roses which matched my bridesmaids' dresses of white and red chiffon and red velvet Juliet caps and muffs. By two o'clock we were ready to set off for what proved to be the strangest and most unconventional wedding I have ever attended.

It was customary in those days in St Thomas' to walk the short distance to church but I could not face the ordeal of walking through the parish in a kind of triumphal procession and, although my mother insisted on walking, my father, my bridesmaids and I went in a hired car. My brother, who was to be best man, was waiting in his car at the station for Edmund's train which was due in from Southampton at 1.45 pm. I arrived at the church with a minute to spare, being highly contemptuous of the convention that a bride should keep her groom waiting. In this case it was the bride, together with her father and the bridesmaids, who were kept waiting in the church porch. Edmund's train was three-quarters of an hour late and he and Syd eventually dashed into church at 2.35 pm. The congregation was getting very restive, turning their heads frequently and muttering to one another. Some of the less generously-minded of them may even have been excited by the prospect of the groom not appearing at all. Poor Edmund was in a dreadful state; he had been on duty all night until 8 am and had scarcely had time to wash properly, least of all to get properly groomed. I gritted my teeth in fury when I heard one guest remark in a high pitched whisper, 'He might have cleaned his boots properly'. Syd could not persuade him to leave his kit bag, bayonet and rifle, in the church porch, in case they were stolen, and since there was not the time to take them back to the car, he advanced up the aisle and propped them against the altar rail! As I quickly followed him up the aisle I was shocked to see that Edmund's father was wearing his inevitable 'deer-stalker' and as the smell of incense pervaded the church he muttered, 'Popery, popery', in a quite audible voice. I suspect that my father agreed with him, but my mother was terribly upset and burst into tears. I think she feared that the Vicar might not proceed with the ceremony. To my mind Mr Gibbs' hat and the 'popery' were by far the worst things that happened and little short of sacrilege, but the rest of the service left a lot to be desired. Not only had Edmund never attended a marriage service before but he was quite dazed and when the Vicar said, 'Repeat after me, "I Edmund Reginald"', he just stood there and said not a word. Again a rustle of expectancy among the congregation. With great patience and understanding Trevor Jalland repeated it and still Edmund remained silent; he told me afterwards that he thought it was a strange coincidence that he and the Vicar shared the same Christian names! You could have heard a feather drop in the Church, let alone a pin, and it wasn't until Syd explained what he was expected to do that the situation returned to normal. But not for long! In talking about the service to the Vicar beforehand I told him how worried I was to have to promise before God that I would obey Edmund because I did not think I always would. He was at pains to point out, although I do not think he altogether approved, that there had been a recent revision of the marriage service and that I could choose not to say 'obey' in which case Edmund would not promise to endow me with all his worldly goods. This was a great relief to me but my Aunt Dorothy, my father's sister, was following the service, line by line, in the Prayer Book, and as I omitted the word 'obey' she called out in triumphant tones, 'There you are, I always said she would never get properly married'.

Our holiday in Torquay had had to be cancelled, of course, but my brother and Winnie offered to move out of their house and our honeymoon was spent in Morrell Avenue. We had lunch with Edmund's parents before he left Oxford for Southampton on the 2.30 pm train. I decided that for the time being I would remain living with my parents and, although I was now a married woman, my father insisted that I was 'in' by 9.30 pm. 'While you live in this house you follow its rules'!

I continued working at the library and was fortunate that my particular post was designated as a 'reserved occupation' which meant that, unlike Joan who was drafted to a munitions factory at Witney and Peggy who joined the Women's Royal Air Force, I could not be called up for 'national service' such as the armed forces, the Woman's Land Army, or munitions. I regularly visited Mrs Munday, now 'Aunt Nance' to me, who looked forward to my visits and made brave attempts to be cheerful while I was there but who found war an almost unbearable strain. It was months after the war had started before we had any news of Gladys but then her mother received a twenty-five word message, through the Red Cross, saying that she was all right, that she was not interned, and we were not to worry. Other letters followed and although they were all painfully brief we did learn of the births of her two daughters and also acquired one very interesting piece of information, namely that she was listening to British radio broadcasts which had been forbidden by Hitler. One of her letters to her mother concluded with the words, 'Give my love to Bruce'. Since Aunt Nance did not know any Bruce she was as mystified by this as I was to a reference to a Mr Bell in a letter I received about the same time. We puzzled over this for many hours and eventually came to the conclusion that she was referring to Bruce Belfrage who was a famous BBC newscaster. We wrote to Mr Belfrage enclosing the letters, begging him not to refer to them but hoping they might interest him. He wrote a charming letter back to Aunt Nance saying that of course he would do nothing to endanger Gladys' safety but that he was enormously encouraged by the information because, although the BBC realised that Hitler would not have imposed the ban had the Germans not been listening to the broadcasts this was the first real evidence they had had.

Rationing was gradually introduced but it did not produce any real problems. As far as food was concerned our diet was healthy but monotonous and there were minor tragedies along the way. My mother-in-law telephoned me one day to say that she had just collected her 'monthly egg' and if I cared to collect mine and bring it round to St Michael's Street we could have supper together. I took it round and after long deliberations we decided to have a poached egg on margarined toast. Sitting at table my mother-in-law, who liked food, gazed fondly at hers before picking up the silver pepper pot and giving it a vigorous shake. Horror of horrors, the top of the pepper pot flew off and that precious egg, the like of which she would not see for another month, was covered in pepper. With tears streaming down her face she flew to the kitchen to pour hot water over it and was not best pleased to hear my hysterical laughter from the dining-room. 'Utility' furniture, and clothes, were made which could be bought on the production of coupons. Some people professed to thinking them hideous but I was not one of these for I thought they were beautifully designed, some very well-known designers being involved, of excellent quality and comparatively cheap. It did not matter to me in the least that my next door neighbour might be wearing an identical suit or dress because a scarf or brooch could give it its own individuality.

Although we heard from Gladys at fairly frequent intervals, there was no news of my French family except for a card from Monique in the early part of 1940. The message on the card simply asked, 'why do you not write to me any more?'. I was upset by this as I had sent three or four letters since the war started and had no replies. I immediately sent her a long letter, but with the fall of France in May 1940, I never heard from her again. Some time after the war I learned that she had died of typhoid during the Italian occupation of Nice and that the 'present whereabouts of her family are unknown'. I was heartbroken by the tragedy and for a long time all I could think was, 'Oh God, I hope she got my letter in response to her card and that she was reassured that I still loved her', but I don't expect she did and I have never been back.

As it dragged on I became increasingly worried about how the war appeared to distort our views and engender hate. I was disturbed by the attitude of former friends of Aunt Nance who distanced themselves from her because Gladys was married to a German; the indiscriminate 'rounding up' and subsequent internment on the Isle of Man of German refugees, many of them Jews, who had come to this country many years before to escape Hitler's purges and were now working in the University; and most of all the way in which people rushed out into the street to cheer our planes setting out for Germany on a bombing mission. I had felt strongly that Hitler and fascism should be opposed but I was horrified at the hate which was generated and the apparent disappearance of all Christian and humanitarian values. Did the people, mostly women, who rapturously cheered in the streets, not realise that with the saturation bombing of such towns as Hamburg and Cologne, men women and children who had had no say in the deliberations and strategies of their leaders would be mercilessly killed? My worries were agonisingly underlined by a girl called Thelma Bristow who came from Bedford to work in the City Library in late 1943 or early 1944. She and her husband were both Quakers and, although he was a conscientious objector, he had volunteered for the Bomb Disposal Squad as he was a qualified engineer. Thelma was on duty in the lending library when the news came that he had been killed while defusing a bomb. Her immediate reaction was not tears, they came later, but a bitter, white-faced condemnation of war and how we all got caught up and destroyed by it. 'John and I wanted no part in this war', she said, 'It was not of our making, but in a war the innocent suffer alongside the guilty whichever side you are on'. For the first time the treacherous thought crossed my mind. Is the concept of a 'just war' a contradiction in terms? Is there no other way to combat evil? It was a thought that returned time and time again but I kept it to myself.

It was with something of a jolt that I reached my twenty-fourth birthday in February 1942 and realised just how quickly the years were passing me by. I was no longer a girl but a young woman. When we married in 1940 we had not contemplated having children during the war but, now that an end to hostilities seemed further away than ever, I began to worry that any children we had would, like me, be born of 'old parents' and I did not want this to be the case. Equally I was determined not to have children while living with my parents: the thought of my father dictating to me as to how his grandchildren, for that is how he would have regarded them, should be brought up sent a cold shiver down my back. I discussed it with Edmund on his next leave and we decided I should look for somewhere to live, away from both families. I dreaded telling my father of our plans for me to leave home but, as was often the case with him, his reaction was unexpected. 'I think its a very sensible idea', he said, 'because you will have to find somewhere to live when Edmund gets back and it will be far more difficult then as so many ex-service men will be looking for homes'.

We could not possibly afford a house and agreed that an unfurnished flat, or rooms, would meet our present needs. Although such accommodation was scarce and relatively expensive I was fortunate in finding exactly what I wanted in a very short time. The depot library I ran at Donnington was housed in the same building as a health clinic. The nurse in charge, Miss Turner, was about to let her three-storied, four bedroomed house at 107 Botley Road because, her mother having recently died, she wanted to move to a smaller house nearer her work. The house was much too big for my needs and certainly for my pocket but it was eventually agreed that the 'front' of the house (living-room, and two bedrooms all on different floors) and similar accommodation at the back would be let separately with joint use of the kitchen and bath, my rent to be twenty-five shillings a week inclusive of rates. I was warned by my friends that such shared accommodation was a recipe for disaster and misery but this did not prove to be the case. One of the girls at the library, Joan Bertholdt, whose home was in Nottingham, asked if I would let the top bedroom to her and this I gladly agreed to as I did not need it. The other tenants were Harold and Olive Wynn-Cuthbert. Olive, whose maiden name was Goddard, was the same age as Syd, and I had known her since I was a child, as at one time her family lived in St Thomas' and her brother Gordon was in nursery class with me. Olive was at that time the organist at St Thomas' Church. From the start we adopted a very practical approach to 'shared accommodation' and, instead of waiting for difficulties, anticipated them! One week Olive would clean the kitchen and hall and I would clean the bathroom and stairs; we switched the tasks the following week. Each weekend we would draw up a 'rota' for the use, the next week, of the kitchen and particularly the cooker, so that we would not be in one another's way. For the last three years we were there, we each had one small child, with only five months' difference in their ages, and this was an added bonus for we 'baby-sat' for one another. Incredible though it may sound we never had a crossword, not even a 'long silence', during the whole of the five years we were together there and Olive has often told me since that they were the happiest years of her married life, for her husband, who was older than she was, died a few years later.

Andrew was born on 23 October 1944 almost four weeks before he was due. I hated pregnancy. I had begun to despair of ever having a child but the moment I knew I was pregnant I was panic stricken. I was not afraid of confinement or changes in my figure; it was the inevitability of it all that terrified me, that this was a condition from which there was no escape. For as long as I can remember I have had a terrible fear of being in situations from which I could not break free. As a child I had two recurring nightmares: one that I would develop scarlet fever or diphtheria and be incarcerated in the Isolation Hospital, the second that I would be sent to prison for a crime which I had not committed. I am ashamed to admit that even as I walked up the aisle to be married I thanked, if not God, then the State, for the Divorce Law! When I informed Mr Skuce of my pregnancy his reaction was typically unhelpful. 'Oh, Miss Cox, or I suppose we must now call you Mrs Gibbs, this is very inconvenient, especially as you are in a "reserved occupation". You might have given some consideration to that'. I refrained from telling him that, at the time, there was no thought of the inconvenience I would be causing him, but it was an effort to bite the words back. As the child was due in mid-November I agreed, if my health permitted, to stay on at the library until mid-October. In fact I was never healthier: no nausea and little other discomfort. I cycled everywhere. Ten days before the birth I cycled to my beloved Wittenham Clumps but I hadn't realised I was cutting the time so close. Labour pains took me by surprise on Saturday 21 October and I went rather reluctantly to the Radcliffe Maternity Home in Walton Street fully expecting to be told to return home and not to be stupid. They took me in at once and after a long confinement culminating in twelve showers, alternatively hot and cold, Andrew was born at 10.30 am on Monday 23 October. Hospital regulations were very strict in those days and I was allowed to be visited by one person only throughout my stay. Edmund, in response to a telephone call from his mother, arrived on the Monday evening, and managed to see me and his son for twenty minutes, before returning to Portsmouth where he was stationed. After that I was allowed no other visitors for the whole ten days I remained in hospital. It was a lonely time and letters were little consolation although I was amused by some of them. Mr Skuce wrote saying he was pleased I was keeping up my reputation for 'always being in a hurry' and one of my library friends asked whether it was true that Andrew had cycled out of the womb.

Some women, I know, are born natural mothers but I wasn't one of them. I was a very bad mother: tense, over-anxious and weighed down by the responsibility of having the entire care of another human being, especially one so small and vulnerable. I tried to breast feed him but it was hopeless, as I communicated my nervousness to him; all I got for my pains was an extremely nasty abscess of the breast. My GP was a woman whose name, sadly, I cannot now remember because I have never known anyone to show such tolerance and understanding to a patient who was forever calling her out unnecessarily. If Andrew had a spot or was sick I was on the telephone to her immediately and she always responded at once. He owes his life to her.

Edmund's father had died in 1942 and since then I had spent much more time with my mother-in-law. One Friday evening in March 1945 we were staying with her for the weekend and Andrew, who was then five months old, was obviously unwell, tossing and turning in his cot and, from time to time, shrieking with pain. The doctor came immediately in response to my call and diagnosed pneumococcal meningitis. She summoned an ambulance and telephoned the Radcliffe for him to be admitted. There was some argument about this, as they were short of beds, and meningitis was a fatal disease in those days. I later learned that she persuaded them to take him in because she was worried about *my* health and wanted to ensure that I was satisfied that everything medically possible had been done for him. I went with him in the ambulance and he was taken into the Leopold children's ward and given a lumbar puncture. Meningitis was confirmed and the ward sister gently asked me whether I realised the gravity of his condition. White-faced and unable to speak I nodded my head, for one of my cousins had died of meningitis. Edmund, who was in Great Yarmouth, was sent for and I asked to be allowed to sit by Andrew's curtained bed which was in a corner of the ward. Someone offered me a cigarette and I chain-smoked throughout that terrible night, watching Andrew have convulsions, and silently praying. Early the following morning a distinguished looking doctor peeped through the curtains and then had a quick word with Sister. She called me out and introduced me to Professor Cairns, later to become Sir Hugh Cairns, the famous neurologist. He asked me if I had ever heard of penicillin. I said, 'Yes, but only very vaguely. I thought I had read that it had been used on soldiers with head injuries'. He told me that I was quite right, that it had been first tried at the end of 1944 on troops in the Middle East but that now they were having tremendous success with it in treating many neurological diseases. Professor Cairns went on to say that it had not yet been used on a child as young as Andrew but, with my permission, he would like to try. 'My only reservation', he said, 'is that if Andrew dies I do not want you to blame me, or pencillin, for his death'. I assured him that I would not do that as Sister had already told me he was not expected to live for longer than twenty-four to forty-eight hours. To my great relief Edmund, when he arrived mid-morning, agreed with the decision I had taken. Andrew was in hospital for many weeks, at one point having to be transferred to Rycotewood Hospital near Thame as there was an outbreak of measles at the Radcliffe. I was allowed to have him home in May. He was very thin and pale but he had survived the meningitis and was later mentioned as 'Baby A' in Hugh Cairns' paper on the use of penicillin in neurology.

Victory in Europe was also celebrated in May and the streets of Oxford, particularly those around Carfax, were full of great cheering crowds. Absent from these celebrations were those who had relatives and friends, either fighting or prisoners of war, in the Far East. I was

not there for I went out very little in those days because, although
Olive and Joan Bertholdt would willingly have baby-sat for me, I was
nervous of leaving Andrew to anyone else's care. However, in August,
I was persuaded by them to accept an invitation to a dance at the RAF
Regiment's Headquarters which were stationed in Sir Arthur Evans'
former home at Boars Hill. I was invited by a young sergeant, Tim
Taylor, whom we had met a year or so before, and who occasionally
'dropped in' for a cup of coffee with us at Botley Road or 'Sunday tea'
at my mother-in-law's. Although his views were, to my mind,
outrageously conservative, he was a gentle, thoughtful boy and, since
he didn't smoke, could always be relied upon to bring me his cigarette
ration. Cigarettes were in very short supply at this time and I had
become since Andrew's illness a fairly heavy smoker.

The date of the dance was 6 August 1945, a date forever on my mind
and in most of the world's mind as well. I left home at 7.30 pm having
given one last anxious look at Andrew and assuring Joan Bertholdt
and Olive that I would not be late. In fact my return was rather more
precipitate than I, or they, had anticipated. In spite of my doubt about
leaving Andrew, it was a good feeling to be dancing again and I was
not short of partners, but just before 9 pm we all retired to the
Sergeants' Mess for a drink and to listen to the news on the radio. I
cannot now remember the exact words used by the newscaster to an-
nounce in measured tones that an atom bomb had been dropped that
day on Japan and the city of Hiroshima had been destroyed. The rest
of the news was drowned as the entire Mess rose to its feet, throwing
caps in the air and wildly cheering. I alone remained in my seat, pale
and trembling. I shall never know whether it was intuition, or whether
it was the suppressed excitement in the announcer's voice, coupled
with a subconsious accumulation of scraps of information about the
splitting of the atom, but I knew for a certainty that the worst crime in
the history of man had been committed and that the world would never
be the same place again. It was, as Fenner Brockway later described it,
a 'blasphemy against the human race'. I told Tim I wasn't feeling well
and would like to go home, refusing his immediate offer to accompany
me because I could not bear to discuss with him, or with anyone else
except Edmund, the atom bomb. I pedalled furiously back to Botley
Road. Olive and Joan were surprised to see me back quite so early but
I said I had a headache, thanked them for looking after Andrew and
went straight to my bedroom. Before I got into bed I looked down at
my small son sleeping peacefully in his cot and wondered what kind of
world he had been born into. I couldn't sleep; I turned restlessly in bed
and longed desperately for Edmund to be there so that he could dispel
my worst fears or share my despair. During those long troubled hours
I came to realise that in a world which held the atom bomb there could
never be any other path for me but pacifism.

But the war was over. Most people received the news of the dropping of the first atom bomb with wild acclaim, believing that the bomb had caused Japan to surrender, although some historians and scientists, notably Professor Blackett, have since argued that the Japanese surrender papers were already in the hands of the Allied Commanders when America, with the agreement of Attlee, took the terrible decision to drop it.

9 · PEACE

In the same way that the horrors of war slowly enveloped us, peace, with one exception, was equally slow in developing and it was a time before we settled down to any kind of normality. For me, the exception overruled everything else, for no longer did I have to live in daily fear of Edmund being bombed or receive news of friends being killed or wounded. Depending on age, length of service, and where they were stationed, men and women of the armed forces were slowly demobbed and returned home. Edmund, now a captain in the Royal Artillery, was retained until 1946 and spent six months of that time in Italy. In 1941 he had spent several months at the War Office and during that time had been successful in passing his final examination in accountancy. It was because he was a qualified accountant that he was transferred to the Royal Engineers and sent to Italy as a member of a team which reported to the Financial Secretary to the British Government on the costing of British Army contracts placed with Italian companies, such as Pirelli. He visited factories in Rome, Turin, Milan and Florence, learned to love the Italian people and felt very deeply about the devastation and poverty in their beautiful country.

In this country a Labour Government, with Attlee as its Prime Minister, had been elected in July 1945, dedicated, among other things, to maintaining full employment and the translation of the Beveridge Report on the Welfare State into the National Health Act of 1947. But living conditions after such a long war were not easy and everything except bad tempers were scarce, food, housing accommodation, and fuel particularly, being in short supply. Food rationing, instead of being abolished as people expected, was extended to include bread, which caused an uproar. My father, bless him, anxious to keep his precious little grandson warm, would trudge down the Botley Road with an old pram and pick up odd pieces of coal which had fallen off the wagons when they were being unloaded at the railway station. My mother, equally concerned, would give us some of her rations, a gesture they could ill afford, but which it was futile for me to argue against. Nor did the weather help. In 1947 it snowed from the beginning of February until the end of March and when the snow melted most of the old parts of Oxford were flooded. The Mayor, Edgar Smewin, a railway-man living in St Barnabas, and Oxford's first Labour Mayor, set up a disaster fund.

People blamed the Government for everything including the weather and my brother used to tell the story of being behind a man cycling over Magdalen Bridge who suddenly had to apply his brakes, skidded on the icy road and fell off his bicycle. As he brushed the snow and ice from his knees he said, 'Bugger this bloody government'. Edmund had not been long home before it became very obvious that he was finding it difficult to adjust to civilian life. He returned to County Hall and was very miserable there, asserting that the work was dull and mononotous and that he was nothing but a glorified office boy. I think the real truth was that he missed the authority he had enjoyed as a commissioned officer during the war and particularly the responsibility of his assignment in Italy. He spent six months with Oxfordshire County Council and then successfully applied for a similar job with Berkshire, but, alas, he was no less miserable there. I began to worry that he would never readjust to civilian life and that I would have a permanently disgruntled man on my hands. I was no less worried about Andrew, who was a delicate child; even his most minor ailments seemed to develop complications and he himself was slow in developing. My fainting fits, which had largely disappeared during my late teens, returned with a vengeance and with them an insidious and quite crippling new fear, that of going out on my own. The fear of fainting became worse than fainting itself although the latter sensation is a horrible one. I always know when I am going to faint and the inevitability of fading away into nothingness and then groping my way back into consciousness terrifies me. As a small child I can remember Mum or Dad saying, 'Quick, our Olive is going to faint, and one or other of them would rush over to me and push my head down between my knees, while the other attempted to force a teaspoon of brandy through my lips. But it never worked and for years the very smell of brandy would make me feel faint. I gave up cycling in case I fainted and fell off my bicycle. I was afraid to take Andrew out for fear he would find himself alone and frightened, with his Mum stretched out horizontally on the pavement. Fortunately he did not lack fresh air because my family and friends, especially my father who adored him, were happy to take him for walks. Stupidly I kept my fears to myself, telling no one and not consulting my doctor. When eventually, in 1954, I was treated for a nervous breakdown, my psychiatrist, Sam Davidson, said that I could have avoided years of misery if I had sought advice then. But I was ashamed of what I considered was a weakness in my character and did not want to be labelled a neurotic. I invented all kinds of ingenious excuses for not going out and if Edmund looked at me quizzically from time to time he kept his thoughts to himself.

In 1947 Miss Turner, who had recently retired, announced that she would like to return to the house on Botley Road. No pressure was put on us to move but after Harold and Olive Wynn-Cuthbert bought a house in Leckford Road we felt increasingly guilty at blocking Miss Turner's return. We could not afford to buy a house, and rented accommodation was impossible to find. I became very worried and upset but I should have heeded a favourite saying of my mother's, 'As one door closes, another one opens'. My mother-in-law quite unexpectedly announced her intention of marrying again. Her husband to be was

Percy Christian, who was a retired farmer, a widower and again twenty years her senior. He had a house in St Margaret's Road, North Oxford and adamantly refused to come and live in St Michael's Street although this was what she really wanted. Faced with Percy's refusal to move in with her, but anxious to retain her lease from Brasenose College, she asked us if we would like to move there. This not only solved our immediate housing problem but solved another problem as well.

For some time Edmund had been wishfully contemplating setting up in practice on his own but he had no premises, no clients and precious little money. Now an opportunity presented itself of turning one of the large rooms in the house into an office and, although I was very uneasy about the insecurity of the whole venture, as I could not bear to see him so miserable in his present job, I suggested we sat down and discussed ways and means of fulfilling his ambition. Since Mr Gibbs' death my mother-in-law had been letting rooms and we could do this, even if on a smaller scale, which would bring in an income while Edmund built up his practice. My father, with incredible generosity, gave him a hundred pounds to 'tide us over' and the die was cast. Edmund became an accountant in private practice and I an Oxford landlady. Rooms in central Oxford were very much in demand and my problem was not in letting accommodation, but having to choose from the applications which poured in. I have since learned that this was not just because of the central position we occupied but because the rents for the rooms were very cheap compared with others; moreover I soon gained a reputation for giving students a 'free meal' when the grants ran out! I could write a book about my lodgers for they included David Adamson of the *Sunday Telegraph*, Brian Walden of Television fame, the present Lord Macintosh of Harringey and Professor Ernest Ambler, a nuclear physicist, now an American citizen, and of such international fame I am told that it is as difficult to arrange an audience with him as it is with the President of the United States. Most of them stayed with us for as long as they were in Oxford and when, after several years, we moved to Iffley Road three of them came with us as they were, by then, part and parcel of the family. One of my lodgers, Thomas Hugh Griffith, I inherited from my mother-in-law. He was in his late eighties, a retired lawyer who, being a Balliol man, had come to Oxford after his London Chambers were bombed. Of extreme Conservative views he once told me that all poor people had ugly faces. I usually held my tongue, in deference to his age, when he embarked on one of these political dissertations, but this was more than socialist flesh and blood could stand. I barked back at him, 'If you care to examine your own face closely in the mirror you will see that such a disadvantage is not restricted to the poor'. He roared with laughter and from that moment on an affectionate respect developed between us. He spent much of the day in the Oxford Union but would often ask in the evenings whether I would do him the honour of taking a glass of port wine with him after dinner. One cold, snowy night, when he was ninety-two, there was a loud banging on our door just before dinner and in a fury I rushed off to open it muttering, 'Why can't people ring the bell?'. There, at my feet, was Thomas Hugh stretched out on the pavement with his stick raised for yet another assault on the door. He had slipped on the pavement and broken his hip. I summoned an ambulance and Edmund and I went with him to the Radcliffe Infirmary, he holding my hand tightly but protesting all the time that there was nothing wrong with him. In the casualty department a young houseman examined him and constantly referred to him as 'Dad'. I held my breath at his insensitivity for I knew at any moment Mr Griffith would react furiously. It happened; although in great pain he sat up slowly on his stretcher and said, 'Young man, since I have never been married you are professing to your own illegitimacy and what is more you are shouting in my good ear'. He made a good recovery but insisted on coming home much too soon. I was very worried the first night he was back and told him that I intended spending the night on a chair in his room; he was horrified and said, 'Spend the night in my room? I have never heard of such a thing. What on earth would your husband say? I should be compromising you!' In fact I spent the night sitting on the stairs outside his room. I did not close my eyes but next morning he said he had had an excellent night. When he could get out again he bought me *The Oxford Dictionary of Quotations* with the inscription on the fly leaf, 'To O.F. Gibbs from T.H.G. Gratiarum Actio Oct-Dec 1952'. It was as much a gift to himself as it was to me for he kept it in his room so that he could consult it when doing the *Times* crossword! But it is now on the bookshelf in our house in Iffley Road where T.H.G. died in 1955, at the age of ninety-six.

Those years in St Michael's Street were hard work but enjoyable. I had a 'daily' Mrs Freda Butler, an absolute gem, but there was still a great deal to do. I was often very tired but having so many people about provided the stimulating company which I would otherwise have missed as I still had this neurosis about going out, and it was becoming worse instead of better, in that I was getting nervous about being anywhere on my own even in the house. I hated the house itself; it was dark with floorboards that creaked and one could hear the rats running about in the walls. I also did not think that it was a suitable environment for Andrew as there were no other children around and he spent most of his time pedalling his tricycle at great speed up St Michael's Street and into the Union where he was a great favourite with Mrs Dubber, the steward's wife. He also held long conversations with John Owen, a colleague of his Uncle Syd's on the Mail and Times, who still writes for the *Oxford Times* under the pen name 'Senex'.

In those days it was a rule of the profession that accountants could not advertise so Edmund had to build up his practice by personal recommendations and it was a slow and often worrying process. I well remember his first clients: Mrs Annetts, a friend of my family who for years had the newsagents shop in the entrance to the Covered Market; Huckin Bros, the builders whom he had met in our 'local' on the Botley Road, the Osney Arms; and Darnell, the plumbers. It is a heartwarming fact that they, or their successors, are still with the firm, Edmund Gibbs and Co., which is now established in a gracious Georgian House in St Giles and boasts five partners, one of whom is our younger son, Simon.

In 1949 our fortunes took a sudden leap forward in a most unexpected way. Syd, who was President of the Headington Football Club, then an amateur club, came to see Edmund, saying in the strictest confidence that the directors had held several meetings and had decided to seek professional status. They were looking for a company secretary and, on Syd's recommendation, had decided to offer the job to Edmund, the fee to be paid to him being £300 a year. Edmund leapt at the offer for it would provide a steady income while his practice developed. What we were too naïve to realise then, was that, also from the practice point of view, his name in print on all the various documents of the Football Club, was one of the best advertisements he could have. He remained company secretary for twenty-five years and it was not so much a job as a way of life for him and, to a lesser degree, for me too.

10 · OXFORD UNITED

We shall always retain an affection for Oxford United and, although Edmund except for being an honorary Vice-President is now no longer connected with the club, we still follow its fortunes closely, over-joyed when it wins, downcast when it loses.

The transition from the Headington Club to Oxford United was far from being a paper transaction; many bitter battles had to be fought before victory was finally achieved. Prejudice was its chief enemy and this was shown in a variety of ways and from different sources. Oxford was in those days, and in some respects still is today, two towns: the Old Oxford of the pre-Billy Morris days and the new Oxford which was born out of his car manufacturing industry. This situation is fur-ther complicated by the division, within the old Oxford, of Town and Gown. Planning problems, which have dogged Oxford United throughout its forty-year history, were never more evident than they were at the very beginning. To obtain the Football Association's as-sent to a change from amateur to professional status it had to get per-mission from the City Council for extensive changes to its ground at the Manor, and it was at this point that all the prejudices rose to the surface. The City Planning Committee of that time was dominated by the University, either as City Council members directly elected by the University, or by Conservatives with University connections. Their attitude towards sport was one of 'gentlemen versus players' and pro-fessionalism was an anathema to them. They were joined on the City Council itself by councillors from the older parts of the City who had a fierce pride in the Oxford City Football Club, for which my brother and my father had played with distinction, although they both welcomed the advent of professional football.

The change, however, was supported by the Labour minority on the City Council whose councillors came mainly from the Headington and Marston, and Cowley and Iffley, wards. The Headington councillors courageously faced the opposition, voiced by the residents living in the area adjoining the Manor Ground, which, although football hooliganism had not then reared its ugly head, was loud and strong. In view of the stand the Labour Group took at that time it has been sad to witness its vacillating attitude towards the club in more recent years. The local press supported those opposing the club and Syd was firmly told that it was not in his interest, as a sports writer, to be involved and that he should sever his connections with Headington. This he did but it was a great blow to him and to the club for he had been one of the cornerstones of the movement to turn professional.

Planning applications were consistently turned down by the City Council but, eventually on appeal, and after an enquiry had been held by an inspector from the Ministry, alterations to the ground, adequate enough to satisfy the Football Association, were agreed. The inaugural meeting to set up the new professional club was held in the Holyoake Hall at Headington in July 1949 and was packed to overflowing. Enthusiastic Headington supporters rushed to buy shares although, because the former directors were anxious to preserve some form of democracy, these were limited to twenty-one for each shareholder. Most of them paid in cash and Edmund came home that night with £1,400 stuffed in his brief-case! The club for many years remained an almost parochial affair. All the original directors, with the exception of Professor George Keeton, an expert on international law, who was a tower of strength to them in their legal battles, were Headington men, most of them coming from old Headington Quarry families. The first chairman was Vic Couling, a boxing promoter who was a former Conservative councillor for Headington and the vice-chairman was Ron Coppock, head of a firm of Quarry stonemasons who later became its chairman and remained in that position for many years. Peter Smith, who worked for the Potato Marketing Board and whose younger brother Jimmy played for the club, brought an element of dynamism to the board as honorary secretary. They held board meetings at least one evening a week and when Edmund set out for one of them I knew not to expect him back until the early hours of the morning for their discussions were interminable.

The adaptations and extensions to the ground were carried out voluntarily, during any God-given daylight hour, by Headington men: Ron Coppock, Frank Lawrence and Percy Cooper among others. Money poured in from an enthusiastic supporters' club, with such names as Gordon Checkley, Freddy Walters, Jim Knapp and Cyril Wiggins springing immediately to mind. When a few years later it became obvious that many of the teams they played did not know where Headington was, and often confused it with Headingley, Leeds it was suggested that the club's name should be changed to Oxford United but all hell was let loose. 'It was *their* club; Oxford had never raised a finger to help them. Why should it pinch their glory now?'. These were some of the questions asked, and rudely answered, but common-sense prevailed and the change of name took place in 1959.

I think that if at that time they could have found a team manager in Headington they would not have bothered to look elsewhere but, in fact, their first player-manager was Harry Thompson, a quiet courteous handsome young man who had played for Wolverhampton Wanderers. After some years he was replaced by Arthur Turner, a very different character, bluff and hearty, who had been with Leeds and Birmingham. But the club went from strength to strength eventually reaching the dizzy heights of Second Division Football. It changed in character too, for 'outside' directors, those not born in Headington, were elected.

Oddly enough, or perhaps it isn't odd, Edmund feels that the 'spirit' behind the club slowly evaporated when the 'Headington' influence disappeared. After many years as chairman Ron Coppock died, at the beginning of the seventies and, a year or two later in 1974, Edmund resigned from his position as company secretary along with several other directors.

It was very much a man's world; even those wives accompanying their husbands to matches were not allowed in the Directors' Room at half-time and that was enough to keep me away from the ground but I went to all the social functions and was in close contact with the players because they came to St Michael's Street on Thursday mornings to be paid. In those days professional football was not the highly paid career it is today and many of the lads were in 'digs' in Headington and looked forward to coming to our home on pay day. I gave them coffee and cake and biscuits and they sat in our sitting-room, reading newspapers or chatting to me about their families, their home towns, and their ambitions. I became very attached to some of them especially the younger ones many of whom came from the North or the Welsh valleys and I suspected were home-sick.

One of the social events I attended was a banquet in the George Restaurant given by Horace Bradley to celebrate one of the team's victories. Horace Bradley, almost certainly the wealthiest director on the board at that time, lived at Barton End, Headington and owned the Cadena Café, and Weeks' Bakery as well as the George Restaurant. It was a splendid occasion attended by many notabilities including the Mayor of Oxford and Sir Harold and Lady Thompson. "Tommy" Thompson (later to become Chairman of the Football Association) and Penelope who, as a University councillor served with me on the City Council for many years, were very good friends of the club. It was a very up-market affair with at least five courses and some of the players looked very ill at ease. I shared the embarrassment of the captain when, after an hors d'oeuvre which was lavish enough to be a meal in its own right, rose to his feet and began making his after dinner speech. But that was nothing to the misery I felt when one of my young favourites on being offered mayonnaise with his cold salmon waved it to one side saying, 'No thanks. I don't like custard with fish'. I wished with all my heart that we could have been in a familiar Headington pub eating fish and chips or steak and onions.

There was great excitement in 1954 when they played Bolton Wanderers in the Cup. On the Saturday afternoon in question I was in my kitchen at Iffley Road, making a pot of tea, when suddenly the silence was shattered by a great roar which I knew must come from the Football Ground and I remember thinking to myself, 'I wonder which one of 'my boys' scored that goal'.

Such was our association with Oxford United. A postscript to that is that Edmund returned briefly to the club in 1982. I had known Bob Maxwell for several years and, shortly after he took over the chairmanship of the club, he telephoned me one lunch-time to ask my advice on several planning matters relating to it. I referred him to Edmund whom he had not then met, saying that he, Edmund, had been the former company secretary and knew far more about the club than I did. As a result of their ensuing conversation Edmund was asked up to Headington Hill Hall and invited by Maxwell to become financial director to the club. It lasted only a year. Edmund found the atmosphere so changed; the team spirit and the democracy appeared to have vanished and, although Edmund would be the first to concede that Bob Maxwell saved the club from extinction and put a great deal of energy and money into its spectacular rise to the First Division, he was not happy there and was glad to leave. I was overjoyed at his decision for I had never known a time before when our family life and arrangements were so much disrupted to meet the sudden whim of the Chairman.

My re-encounter with the club was a happier one. In May 1985 Roger Dudman, a close friend of ours, was elected Lord Mayor and, his wife having died many years before, he invited me to be his Lady Mayoress – rather more for my experience than for my charm I suspect! One of the highlights for me of this year of office was accompanying him to Wembley in 1986 to see Oxford United win the Milk Cup. Edmund preferred to watch it at home on television but Andrew, Simon and my two grandsons, Mark and Geoffrey, piled into FC1, the Mayoral car, to make the momentous trip to London. Henry (Ollenbuttel), one of the Town Hall staff, who was a fervent and faithful supporter of the club, at our invitation, came with us. All Oxford, as well as all Headington, appeared to be on the road, and the excitement reached fever pitch. As we passed coaches, minibuses, vans, cars and motor-bikes with yellow and blue OUFC banners streaming behind them we tooted our horn in salute and the little boys vigorously waved their flags. We won and, with hoarse throats but the satisfied grins of cats who have tasted the cream, we returned to Oxford acknowledging all our 'fellow victors' on the way. This time I had been invited into the Directors' Room but whether this indicated a more progressive outlook or was in deference to my rank I thought it better not to enquire. Roger gave an official reception in honour of the club and the Cup was held aloft, for the hundreds of cheering supporters thronging St Aldates, on the very balcony from which the Munich By-election result had been announced almost fifty years before when Bob Maxwell was a young man in Czechoslovakia.

11 · THE BOYS

Simon was born in 1951 and, as with Andrew, I experienced no problems during pregnancy except, yet again, a fierce desire to 'escape'. He, too, decided his Mum was not to be kept waiting and at 8.30 am on 18 July, the day forecast for his birth, I had mild labour pains. Since we had decided that the birth would take place at home, and not in hospital, Edmund telephoned our GP, Dr Sweet, who arrived about half an hour later, gave me a brisk examination, said that he would inform the midwife although it was unlikely the birth would occur before the evening and advised me to carry on normally. That was fine until my mother-in-law, having been telephoned by Edmund, arrived to take charge, and every vestige of normality flew out of the window. Mrs Christian said I must not dust, I must not sweep, I must not wash the dishes, for fear of harming the baby. When it got to the point where I was almost afraid to breathe in front of her I exploded and said, to her shocked amazement, that I intended getting out of my chair and carrying on as usual. Fortunately the midwife, Nurse Miller, arrived at this moment and confirmed my view that exercise would do me good. As soon as she had left, promising to be back at 5.30 pm, Mrs Christian resumed where she had left off, regaling me with an unending flow of 'old wives' tales'. I thought I should go mad and contemplated telephoning Edmund, whose office was now in Broad Street, but I did not want to worry him, so I took all my courage in both hands and decided to walk the few steps to the Northgate Tavern, our local, where I occasionally accompanied Edmund for a drink.

It was the hottest day of the year and as the saloon bar was quite empty I sank thankfully into a seat and ordered a Pimm's No 1. As Percy Chapman, the landlord, put it down in front of me he said, 'And how are you today, my dear? I suppose it won't be long now'. I replied, 'No, Percy, as a matter of fact it has already started'. The effect on him was electric; he snatched the glass from my hand, slices of fresh fruit and a glacé cherry spilling all over the table, and, red in the face, shouted, 'You get back home then; where you ought to be'. I was aghast for he was normally a quiet, dear man and I tried to explain to him that my mother-in-law was making me nervous. 'You are nervous, are you?', he thundered, 'and what do you think I am? I have had one baby born in this pub and I don't want another'. I knew what he was talking about, for all of us, at one time or another, had heard the harrowing story of the baby which was born in the cloakroom of his pub during the war, and I could only think of replying feebly, 'But that one was illegitimate, Percy, this one is legitimate'. 'It makes no difference whether its legitimate or illegitimate', he yelled back, 'It makes the same sort of mess. Now be off with you'. I crept tearfully home to be faced with Mrs Christian demanding to know where on earth I had been. Economical with the truth I replied, 'For a walk'. Next morning, beside the milk bottles in the crate outside our front door were two bottles of champagne with a label attached saying 'With love from Percy'. Edmund, too, was later deprived of a much needed drink.

The day dragged on; five-thirty came and went and so did the labour pains, and the midwife arrived at 8.30 pm resigned to staying the night. It was *so* hot. Edmund looked in at my room at regular intervals; he was white-faced and obviously as disturbed by his mother's dire forebodings as I had been. At 9 pm I advised him to go down to 'Percy's' for a drink and with only a token resistance he went. Fifteen minutes later the labour pains returned in force and feeling very sorry for myself I weepingly told Nurse Miller I wanted him back. 'Where is he?', she said (I don't think she had a very high opinion of men) and on being told that he was at the Northgate she marched down to fetch him. Edmund says he will never forget the moment when the bar door was flung open and the nurse, red-faced and with her sleeves rolled up to the elbows, advanced towards him, removed his glass from his hand, stood it on the bar, and with a sharp tap on his shoulder said 'Home'. Simon was born at 3.45 am on 19 July and much to my relief was a perfectly healthy baby with all his fingers and all his toes.

The following day I received a telegram from Mr Griffith, who had gone to stay with friends, saying, 'Congratulations. I am happy to know that you have been safely delivered of a male child'. Male child indeed! I had desperately wanted a girl and was very disappointed, but when, with the exception of Edmund and Andrew, the rest of the family expressed disappointment that he was not a girl I became fiercely defensive of his sex. Andrew was overjoyed and confided in me, 'I am so glad it is a boy, Mummy, I shall be able to take him fishing'. That, for me, decided his name, Simon: Andrew and Simon the fishers of men. Midge, Mrs Butler's fifteen-year-old niece, was engaged as a resident 'nanny' and stayed with us until she got married six years later.

No two children could have been more different in character than our two sons. Andrew was timid and compliant while Simon was self-assertive and aggressive. The two following recollections probably illustrate this difference between them more clearly than any attempt to describe them. One morning at breakfast Andrew, who was then about six years old, was mumbling something to me and I said, 'For goodness sake, Andrew, empty your mouth before you speak'. His response was immediate and literal; he spat all that he was eating into his hand, said what he wanted to say, and then crammed it all back into his mouth! Some years later Simon, at around the same age, found an empty cement bag which the builders had left in the garden and filled it with water. With horror I watched him as he slowly swung it backwards and forwards; I knew what he intended to do and he knew that I knew. We gazed at one another as if under hypnosis and at last I found the words to say 'Don't you dare, Simon'. He did; and the cement bag crashed through the French window scattering glass and water all over the sitting-room carpet and causing thirty pounds' worth of damage. For the first, and last, time in his life I slapped him and, screwing up his face to hold back his tears, he still managed to poke his tongue out at me. I sent him to bed but presently the sitting-room door opened a crack and Simon, knowing I was apt to faint at the sight of blood, said in a low sepulchral voice 'Bl-oo-ood' and flew back up the stairs.

On those frequent occasions when he drove me to the limits of exasperation I would remind myself of the comparisons always made when I was a child between my brother and me; and always in Syd's favour. Moreover even at the time, and still more since, I have realised that I was much too protective of Andrew, attempting to put myself as a shield between him and anything that threatened, which was not fair, or of benefit, to either of them. Fortunately Simon adored Midge, who spoiled him outrageously, and Edmund was always around to put a check on my excessive preoccupation with Andrew's health.

Nowadays I find it not only satisfying but enormously reassuring to hear both our sons reminiscing with one another about their childhood and recounting to their children various stories from the past for, in spite of my misgivings, it is quite obvious that those were very happy times for them. I love watching my grandchildren listen, wide-eyed, to their parents telling them of all the adventures and mishaps which befell the Gibbs family in the fifties and early sixties and particularly those about holidays and 'the Car'. In the time-honoured style of story-telling all these stories begin with 'Do you remember?'.

Listening to them I found it something of a shock to realise that they regarded us as slightly 'dotty' (quite different from their friends' parents), and that Dad was a much kinder and more tolerant person than Mum. Examples of my 'cruelty' were that I made them sit on the beach in a howling gale until they were blue with cold as 'the sea air was good for them', and the time when Andrew, bidding 'goodbye' to his friends at the end of a holiday, walked backwards into the swimming pool, and the only sympathy he got from me was an exasperated 'Why on earth did you do that, Andrew, you know all your clothes are packed?'. They are never tired of telling the story of Edmund playing cricket on the common, slipping as he ran to retrieve a ball and rolling down the sandy slope to be run over by a perambulator as he lay outstretched on the promenade. Nor do they need any urging to talk of the time when he forgot to pack his swimming trunks and was determined to find the cheapest pair he could as a temporary replacement. He found them in the Lee Emporium at a cost of half a crown. They looked fine when he first put them on but when he re-emerged from the sea after a very short time the sight that met our eyes was quite extraordinary: the legs of the trunks had reached calf length and the elastic round the middle was biting into his waist almost cutting him in two. Try as he might he could not get out of the wretched things until I resourcefully took a pair of nail scissors from my hand-bag and cut him free. Needless to say all the people on the beach, including the boys and me, were helpless with laughter as he stumped angrily away.

One night on holiday when I was too hot to sleep I looked out of the window across the water at what I thought were the lights of Ryde on the Isle of Wight. Suddenly, to my horror, they began to move and, in a panic, I woke Edmund and the boys urging them to get dressed quickly as there had been an earthquake or something. Edmund looked out and then said reassuringly to Andrew and Simon, 'It's all right; it isn't an earthquake and it isn't the Isle of Wight; it's the *Queen Mary* sailing into Southampton Water'.

Simon is fond of warning his children that there is some danger about going out with Granny as she is accident prone. This reputation stems from the time when I put, what turned out to be, a damaged coin in the turnstile at the Woman's Convenience on the sea front and thereby jammed the lock. We rattled it, we banged it, we poked hair grips into it, but nothing would open that gate. Edmund hastily charged off to find the 'council offices' leaving the boys with me and they were as scarlet with embarrassment as I was, and just as frightened, when the women behind me in the queue, who were now 'in extremis', hurled insults and threats at me. Not long ago, Simon accompanied me to a banquet where, half way through the meal, a false tooth which I had recently acquired worked loose and I was afraid I was going to swallow it. With what I thought was great presence of mind I mumbled my predicament to Si; I told him I was going to drop my napkin on the floor and that he was to leave me to retrieve it. While getting down to my napkin I replaced my tooth at the same time which I thought was a marvellous feat of ingenuity. Simon was not so impressed; he was set-faced as I resumed my seat and he hissed in my ear, 'Oh Mum, you don't change do you? I have heard of people being under the table with drink but never before with teeth'. Obviously for him the 'old Mum' was no different from the 'young Mum' who deliberately put bent pennies in machines just to embarrass him!

Practically all of their holiday stories relate to Lee-on-Solent in Hampshire which is hardly surprising since we spent ten consecutive years there; one before Simon was born and nine afterwards. It could hardly be described as a fashionable sea-side resort; it had no large hotels and only one or two small ones but there were two good pubs, the Victoria Arms and the Inn by the Sea, and several restaurants of varying attractions. It boasted few amenities other than a modest open-air swimming pool on the front and a splendid putting green on the recreation ground at the back of the town which also housed, thanks to Hampshire County Council, an excellent Branch Library.

Its main public attraction, and depicted on all the picture postcards for sale, was Lee Tower, a hideous construction built to resemble a lighthouse, painted a glaring white, with a small amusement arcade underneath it. Sometime ago it disappeared; whether it was deliberately demolished or was destroyed by an Act of God I don't know but in either case it was an entirely justifiable action.

Lee had a pebbled beach almost permanently polluted by tar from the many tankers, and possibly from some of the large liners like the *Queen Mary*, and the *Canberra* which made their way through the Solent to Southampton Dock. It was a very popular place for people with small yachts and there was an impressive Yacht Club on the front but, other than these, few holiday makers stayed there although there were often day trippers arriving in coaches to stare at that dreadful tower. Its original 'village' population had been swelled by a number of elderly, often sea-faring people, who chose to retire there, and the establishment of HMS *Daedalus*, a branch of the Fleet Air Arm, but in all it numbered only between two and a half and three thousand inhabitants.

We chose it in the first place because of the offer of free accommodation. In 1949 Percy Christian, Edmund's step-father, bought a large house there on the sea front at Marine Parade West, with a splendid view over the Solent. He divided it into two large flats; the ground floor was let permanently, mainly to service people, and the first floor which had a large living-room, two bedrooms and a spacious glass-shuttered balcony, in addition to a bathroom and kitchen, he kept as a holiday retreat for him and Rose or any other member of the family who wanted to use it. We could never go on holiday until after the Annual General Meeting of Oxford United but, since that was usually at the end of July or the beginning of August, it fitted in well with the boys' school holidays and we rarely went for less than a month. As the boys often chose to sleep on the balcony we were also able to have occasional visitors from Oxford. I shall never forget the week my parents stayed with us; my father had never had a 'sea-side' holiday before and my mother was enchanted by a visit to Portsmouth and its Guildhall although she was shocked and moved to tears at the destruction, by enemy action, of the area around the docks which she had known as a small child.

We had our main meal out, but otherwise ate in the flat and everyone was allocated a 'task' so that housework and cooking were reduced to a minimum for me. The boys spent most of the day on the beach as, although the Solent has two tides, the bathing is safe, and in the evenings we often went to the putting green. As a special treat each year we made at least one trip to the Isle of Wight which the boys thought was a tremendous adventure. On wet days we sampled the more urban pleasures of Fareham, Gosport and Southampton. It amuses Edmund to tease me that, once when we were in Gosport, I said as I sheltered under my umbrella, 'It does seem to rain a lot here' and he looked at me in astonishment and said, 'Well that's because we only come here when it's wet'. After Percy's death in 1953 the house was sold and, because of my politically worrying reluctance to personal change, we rented houses there for several more years, becoming, on our annual visit, almost part of the community and greeted warmly, by name, in the shops, pubs and restaurants. However, as the boys grew older and Andrew was in his teens, I thought, since we could now well afford it, it was time we took them somewhere else where we, ourselves, could enjoy the comforts of a hotel. We spent two holidays at Exmouth, in Devon, but the following year when I asked Andrew and Simon where they would like to go, they enquired anxiously, 'Mum, would you mind very much if we went back to Lee?'. They had inherited their mother's conservatism!

Once we had decided to go to Lee-on-Solent the difficulty was to know how to get there. We had no car and I was in a state of nervous collapse at the thought of travelling on a train or coach because, short of pulling the train's communication cord or shouting at the coach driver to stop, there was no way of escape from these vehicles. I had a lurking suspicion too that, even if I managed to get to Lee, I should have to stay there for the rest of my life because nothing would persuade me to make the return journey. Edmund suggested that we should ask friends to take us, explaining my problems to them, but I would have none of it for I was adamant that my neurosis should not be disclosed and discussed with anyone. Poor Edmund; his patience was inexhaustible and, when I finally went for psychiatric help, Sam Davidson told me that he was uncertain as to which one of us needed treatment as Edmund looked far worse than I did.

After many anxious calculations we finally decided we could just afford to buy a second-hand car provided it did not cost more than a hundred pounds. Edmund had passed his driving test before the war and had some driving during it, but by no stretch of the imagination, could he be described as mechanically minded. As for me I had then and still have an irrational fear, and terrified loathing, of all machinery. It probably stems from my childhood days when I was taken to visit my father at his place of work and all those monstrous black printing machines were in ear-splitting operation. Try as I may I cannot overcome the sensation that a machine controls me and not I the machine. The vacuum cleaner assumes a will of its own, leading me around the room, and the flex of the electric iron seems intent on strangling me. One generous, but misguided, friend once gave me a steam iron, with disastrous consequences; it hissed in my ear and I dropped it on to an expensive cocktail dress I was pressing and burned a great hole in it. I long for the days of my mother's wooden hand-operated mangle and her heavy flat iron. No one appreciated Charlie Chaplin's film *Modern Times* more than I did and I am sure that had I been around at the time I would, for all the wrong reasons, have been a leader of the Luddite Rebellion.

So the scene was set for any shark which cared to come along and it came in the shape of a new client of Edmund's. He had a double-barrelled name and a business on the verge of bankruptcy, but we were not aware of the latter because his books had not yet been audited. On hearing that we were looking for a second-hand car he told Edmund that he was about to buy a new car but had to sell his present one first as he had not room for two cars in his garage. He waxed lyrical about the car he wanted to sell: 'It was a quality car; a Lanchester, in excellent condition'. It also had a fluid fly wheel (whatever that means). The asking price was £150 but in spite of the fact that we told him we could not afford so much he insisted on bringing it round to St Michael's Street for us to look at it. It was certainly a very elegant looking car: large, upright and black, the type of car much favoured by Queen Mary and funeral directors. He and Edmund went round the block in it and it seemed to run perfectly too, but we reluctantly told him that we really could not buy it as we had not got one hundred and fifty pounds. We ought to have seen the red light at the speed with which he said that, as a special favour to us as he liked us, he would let us have it for one hundred and twenty pounds and, believing it to be a bargain we could not miss, we agreed; he asking for a cash payment. Wally Johnston, the caretaker of the City of Oxford High School for Boys, and his wife Marion, who were friends of ours, allowed us to garage it, without payment, at the back of their house in New Inn Hall Street. Apart from one or two very short runs we did not use it until we set out for our holiday at Lee and then its disadvantages became only too apparent. The petrol consumption was staggering: it did only twelve to fifteen miles to the gallon. Moreover if the speed exceeded twenty miles an hour we had to wait at least half an hour for the engine to cool down. The journey which was only seventy-two miles took us over four hours to complete. On the way home, as we were coming down a hill into Newbury, the car hit a pothole; all the doors flew open and we were lucky not to lose Andrew who was in the back on his own. Thereafter I would not go out in that infernal machine unless all the doors were roped together for safety which made other motorists yell derisory remarks as they overtook us. I tried to look as disdainful as Queen Mary but I had neither the face, the figure, nor the toque to get away with it. After a couple of years its condition deteriorated to a point where it was no longer safe on the road and we asked Edmund's mother if it could be housed in her garage at St Margaret's Road until we could dispose of it. Its end was as ignominious as its life with us had been. Another client of Edmund's, an antiques dealer, very far from bankruptcy, was interested in 'veteran' cars and asked if he could have the garage keys to have a look at it, to which we gladly agreed. He returned, much impressed, to ask for the keys of the car itself as he thought he might take it. Take it he did, together with the backdoor of my mother-in-law's garage, her washing line with the clothes still on it, and part of her rear garden wall. Edmund said plaintively afterwards, 'Well I did warn him about the fluid fly wheel' so that must have been a significant factor in the eventual demise of that unfortunate car.

12 · POLITICS

Throughout this period my interest in politics had not waned, although any active participation in them was severely curtailed by the crippling disability of being unable to go out anywhere on my own. I had fierce arguments with Ernest Ambler who thought that shooting was too good for Klaus Fuchs, the spy, who worked at the Atomic Research Centre at Harwell and was arrested at Steventon, near Abingdon, and sentenced to fifteen years imprisonment in 1950. As a nuclear physicist Ernest's views were understandable but I believe Fuchs was sincere when he said he believed world tension would be lessened, and not intensified, by a sharing of nuclear knowledge among nations. However, at a time when the cold war was reaching a crescendo and the general view was that we could not live in peace without a vast increase in armaments it was inevitable that the public attitude should be that 'our' spies were heroes and 'theirs' were sub-human. Spy fever was even more intense in the United States where the Rosenbergs were sentenced to death in 1951 for spying. It was unheard of for the western world to execute spies for peace-time activities but, in spite of world wide protests, the sentence was never commuted and the Rosenbergs went to the electric chair in 1953, leaving behind two small children. I love this country, its customs and its traditions, with a singular passion, and would not choose to live anywhere else in the world, but 'patriotism', as Edith Cavell said, 'is not enough'.

With some minor, and one major exception, I had then, and still have, a tremendous admiration for the courage and single-mindedness of the Labour Governments of 1945-51. Without looking over their shoulders to see whether the legislation they were enacting would 'lose them votes', which is almost endemic among present politicians, they put into operation their electoral promises of making Britain a more just and equal society. For me, of no less importance was the determination with which they gave self-rule to India, for this was evidence of their belief in the brotherhood of man, irrespective of colour, creed or race and a principled and spirited rejection of the jingoism of Empire. I thought they were mean-minded not to give the child allowance of ten shillings a week for the first child. They ought to have been more in touch with poorer families and therefore to know that the first child is always the greatest strain on the family budget; prams, cots and other necessities can be passed on to the second. My Mum could have given them a lesson on the prime importance of a pram!

My over-riding concern with the Attlee Government – and it is difficult to assess where the blame lay, with Attlee or his cabinet, since reports on this vary so much – was its policy on nuclear weapons and its decision to manufacture the British independent deterrent. I had been appalled at Attlee's acquiescence in the dropping of the Bomb on Hiroshima but prepared to believe that he did it not knowing the fearful consequences of such an action. Einstein himself had said, 'Had I known I would have been a locksmith', and I gave Attlee the benefit of the doubt. However, after 1946 it was obvious, not least from the debates in the House of Commons on Civil Defence, that with nuclear weapons the difference was qualitative, not simply quantitative, from any weapon which had preceded them. Never before had there been a situation where after the 'all clear' had sounded, one could not count the dead and the dying, for the immediate effect of radiation was not obvious; moreover children, who had not yet been born, would be affected by it. All those intuitive, though seemingly irrational, fears I had faced on that terrible night of 6 August 1945, were coming true. It is fair to comment that, at this point, no other British political party, including the Communist party, was against the independent deterrent, although a few individuals, mainly churchmen, scientists and intellectuals, spoke out against any defence policy which was based on the use, or threatened use, of nuclear weapons; these were by no means all pacifists for they knew that these were weapons of mass suicide as well as of mass destruction and that their use could pollute the earth and adversely affect future generations.

There was also within the Parliamentary Labour Party, probably due to Ernie Bevin's influence within the Cabinet, a quite frightening anti-communist attitude and, although this never sank to the depths of the McCarthy 'Un-American Activities' committee, there was certainly some evidence of political persecution. One evening towards the end of 1949 or the beginning of 1950 a bowler-hatted detective from the Oxford CID called to see Edmund at home and asked him whether he knew that the wife of a young man who was working for him was a communist. 'No', replied Edmund, 'and why should I be interested?'. 'Well', the detective said, in a most unpleasant tone, 'We thought you might want to sack him'. 'Certainly not', said Edmund, white with anger, 'In the first place I do not believe in guilt by association, and secondly, since communism is not yet illegal in this country, if he himself were a communist I would not sack him unless his political views began to interfere with his work; our visitor, who did not appear to be very intelligent, looked furious and a few days later we learned he had visited a business friend of Edmund's and intimated to him that Edmund, himself, was a communist sympathiser. In the late 1950s when the City Council was split, though not on party lines, on the question of whether the National Union of Fascists should be allowed to hold a meeting in the Town Hall, I voted for permission to be given but I doubt anyone dubbed me a 'Nazi sympathiser' whether on that account.

It was at this time too, that I came to the conclusion that capital punishment was nothing short of state murder. From the age of eleven or twelve years I hated reading in the newspapers that an execution was to take place. So affected was I that on the night before an execution was to be carried out I would turn the clock to the wall so that in the morning I would not know it was 8 am and the hanging was actually taking place. Even then I slept fitfully and could not wrench my thoughts away from the man in the condemned cell awaiting such a horrible death. At sometime in my teens an execution took place at Oxford Prison and for years afterwards I always avoided walking up New Road believing that, as the notice saying that the execution had been carried out was pinned on the front gate of the prison, it was behind that gate it had happened. Nearly a quarter of a century later I learned that the execution cell was at the back of the prison and, in avoiding New Road, I had walked straight past it. In spite of the genuine horror I felt I am ashamed to admit that I was not then opposed to capital punishment, believing it was a deterrent although I did not share my father's Old Testament fanatical belief in an 'eye for an eye and a tooth for a tooth'.

This paradox was resolved for me in 1952 when Bentley and Craig were tried and found guilty of the murder of a policeman and Bentley was sentenced to death. The police officer had actually been shot by Craig but, since he was under eighteen years of age, a death sentence on him could not be imposed. The so-called damning evidence against Bentley, who was nineteen years of age and of low intelligence, was that he had shouted to Craig just before the fatal shot, 'Let him have it, Chris' although his defence lawyers submitted that it meant 'Give him (the policeman) the gun'. It was a case which shocked not only the abolitionists but a great many other people in this country who, in other circumstances, believed as I did that the death penalty was a deterrent. Sidney Silverman, the Labour Member of Parliament for Nelson and Colne, who was not in favour of the death penalty, was particularly horrified by this case. He fought for Bentley's life right up to the moment of the boy's death in January 1953 and kept the House sitting throughout the night before the execution in an heroic, but vain attempt to secure a reprieve. The whole of the period of that trial was a nightmare for me. I wrote letters to the paper, signed petitions, and sent telegrams to Sidney Silverman. I did not really believe that Sidney Silverman could fail and I was devastated to learn from the radio at ten minutes past eight on that fateful morning that Bentley, poor stupid boy, had been executed. Edmund, holding me as I wept, asked me what I kept saying, and through my tears said, 'Father forgive them'. As I had followed the trial so closely I heard all the cogent arguments against the death penalty and the theory of deterrence, and I and, I believe, many thousands more were not only convinced that Bentley should not have died but that there was no Christian or moral defence for the retention of the death penalty.

It has never failed to amuse me that, on many occasions when I have been sharing a political platform with other speakers, one of them has smitten his chest and announced to the audience in ringing and self-congratulatory tones that he has been a member of the Labour Party since birth, or a life-long Trade Unionist. This never fails to conjure up for me an irresistable mental picture of party cards being issued in the labour wards of our hospitals and shawl-wrapped Trads Unionists being carried to the font and baptised into the true faith by a near-Marxist minister, or even bishop! I have no such credentials for, although I have been a socialist for as long as I have been able to think for myself, until I reached my mid-thirties I did not feel the need, and certainly had no desire, to join a political party. I felt, and on occasions I still feel, that no reasonably intelligent and independently-minded person can honestly subscribe to all the dogma and doctrinaire policies of one particular party.

Moreover I have a suspicion, and it has not diminished over the years, that political parties and other organisations often become more important to their membership than the aims and principles for which they were first set up. One is constantly warned against doing this, or doing that, in case it loses 'us' votes or loses 'us' members. Not long before Hugh Gaitskell, the Leader of the Labour Party, died I was having dinner with him and his daughter Julie, who was up at Oxford, and I was horrified when he said during a discussion on education, 'Yes, of course I believe in the abolition of private education, Olive, but the electorate is not yet ready for it'. Jack Jones of the Transport and General Workers once said, 'I do not want power unless it is to achieve those things in which we believe', a philosophy with which I entirely agree. I am not denying that there are times when half a loaf is to be preferred to no loaf at all, especially in the interests of the less privileged members of our society, but I do think we should never lose sight of our long term objectives and I worry about the emasculation of party policy in order to gain power. Of the two definitions of politics 'the language of priorities' and the 'art of the possible' I prefer the former.

Nor am I happy at the personal hostility with which many politicians treat members of other political parties, regarding them as 'untouchables'. A few years ago I accompanied Edmund, who was then National President of the Association of Certified Accountants, to a regional dinner in Southampton, at which he was the guest speaker. During his speech he paid a gracious tribute to the guest of honour who was a woman and the city's Deputy Mayor. He added, 'I would also like to extend a very warm welcome to her husband as I understand the problems of husbands with wives in public positions. No sooner, with a sigh of relief, did I give up being the Lady Mayoress of Oxford, than my wife went off and got herself made Leader of the Opposition on Oxfordshire County Council'. At the end of the dinner the 'chained

figure' bore down on me and exclaimed, 'I always thought Oxfordshire County Council was Conservative'. 'It is', I replied. 'But your
hubby said you were Leader of the Opposition', she countered. 'I am',
I said, 'I am a socialist'. At this point one of her chins dropped down
on to her chest and she was bereft of speech. Politely enough I continued, 'You look surprised'. 'I am', she replied, 'I am absolutely astounded. I thought you was a lady'. That was too much for me and as I
turned on my heel I cut her short with 'And that, Madam, is a mistake
I would never have made as far as you are concerned'. All of us and
especially those with strong political views should remember that a
democracy cannot exist without opposition; it will become a dictatorship either of the right or the left and, if for no other reason, one should
respect it even if not agreeing with it. I, too, am not without sin in this
respect and only God knows how many times I have asked Him to
forgive me for being inexcusably offensive to my known 'bête noire'
on the Oxford political scene.

However, in 1952, as the result of a sequence of events, those
doubts, if not entirely resolved, were at least cast to one side and I joined the Oxford City Labour Party. At the end of 1951 Florence
Horsbrugh, the Conservative Minister of Education, told local
authorities that their Government grant was to be cut by five per cent,
adding the usual rider that they must achieve this cut without damag-
ing the essential fabric of education. The immediate response of the
Tory controlled County Borough of Oxford was to close five nursery
classes in South and West Oxford. Most of these classes had been in
existence for more than fifty years and one of them was St Thomas'
Nursery. A group of Mums, who had been in this nursery with me and
who now had their own children attending it, called to see me at our
home in St Michael's Street one morning and begged me to go down to
St Thomas' School that afternoon, and put their case against closure to
a group of councillors who had agreed to meet them there. They stood
in some awe of councillors and thought I was better equipped to speak
on their behalf. The two doing the most talking were Mrs Ashmall and
Mrs Van Gucci who as Edna Webb and Stella Faulkner had been close
friends of my childhood.

I got more and more agitated as they went on talking. I knew I could
not possibly go down to the school and confront those councillors; I
should faint and then what would happen? In the end I told them I was
terribly sorry but I really did not think I would do their cause any good
as I knew nothing at all about it and it would be much more sensible for
them to find someone who did. 'Who?' they demanded in their usual
no-nonsense St Thomas' fashion. 'Who knows more about the school
and the parish than you do?'. I was not to be persuaded, or rather, I
could not be persuaded for I was by this time consumed with fear.
Their faces made obvious their disappointment and I knew that disappointment to be partly because they would have to present their own

case, but much more because I had 'let them down'. I suffered agonies after they left; I could imagine them discussing me and asking themselves, 'What has happened to Olive? Doesn't she care? Or is it that she now regards herself as superior to us and does not want to be reminded that she comes from St Thomas'.

I became more and more depressed as the morning wore on and at lunch-time I could not touch any food. Suddenly Edmund put his knife and fork down and said in a voice half way between pity and exasperation, 'For goodness sake, Olive, pull yourself together. You have told them you are not going so what is worrying you now?'. 'I feel so awful', I replied, 'they will think I have let them down'. 'Well', Edmund replied bluntly, 'that is exactly what you have done isn't it?'. 'But I can't go down there', I wailed, 'you know I can't'. 'I know nothing of the kind', he said, and then, softening a little, he added, 'Now look, if you will go I will take an hour off this afternoon and come with you, but I will not come into the school. I will wait in your parents' house and if you are taken ill I can be with you in a couple of minutes'.

I knew I had to accept this offer or live with the knowledge that those childhood friends of mine, for whom I had a great affection and respect, would have little affection and certainly no respect for me.

The meeting was timed for three o'clock and, as it was Midge's afternoon off, we took Simon with us in his carry-cot and I left him and Edmund with my mother. I was so frightened I was trembling as I walked through the school gate but the relief on the faces of the assembled mums and the warmth of their welcome did much to steady my nerve. By way of explanation I said, 'I thought I would come because, even though I know nothing about it, I was also against closing our nursery'. Their confidence in me was overwhelming. 'She was always a fighter', they said to one another, 'she'll floor them'. I thought, as I was introduced to the councillors when they arrived, that it was far more likely that I would be the one to be floored, and in more senses than one!

Representing 'authority' was the Conservative chairman of the Primary Education Sub-Committee, Councillor Lionel Harrison, and three of the West Ward Conservative councillors, Councillor Ernie Mott, Councillor Stewart Duke and Councillor Leonard Walker. The councillors opened the batting and I was appalled as much by the way in which they 'talked down' to the assembled parents, as by the rubbish they talked. Councillor Harrison enlightened us with the facts: the economic needs of the country justified this cut; nursery classes were the only item in the Education Budget which could possibly be cut; the classes had only been introduced during the 1939-45 war. The three other councillors supported him with such profound observations as 'young children are much better off being looked after by their mothers than by being at school. As the compulsory school age is five years old then obviously that is the right age for them to go to school'.

I was so angry every vestige of fear left me as I tore into the attack. 'Since I went to nursery class in 1920 at the age of two years and my brother, at the respectable age of three years in 1908, then it must be the Boer War and not the last war you were referring to. If children were better off being cared for by their mothers then why had the Council only reached this decision when cuts had to be made?

Moreover why did royalty, and others who could afford it, employ 'nannies' to look after their children? Were they aware that the majority of the children attending St Thomas' nursery class lived in the Buildings and, unlike royalty and the rich, had no gardens in which to play? Wasn't it true that the Council could offset this cut and leave the classes open at a cost of only a farthing extra on the rates (A fact I had gleaned from Edmund on the way down)?. They had no answers to these questions and left, promising nothing further than to report back to the Education Committee, though more accurately I suspect, to their political masters.

I was exhausted at the end of this, but happy: I knew I had not yet won the battle of the nursery class but I had won back the affection and respect of St Thomas', and I had not fainted. I returned to my mother's and she made tea for me and the other mums who dropped in to discuss the next steps we should take. Flushed with triumph and relief, I did not notice that Edmund, who was there when I got back from the school, had slipped away during these discussions. Panic returned but Edna and Stella were only too anxious to walk back home with me and carry Simon in the carry-cot. As soon as they had left I demanded to know of Edmund why he had left me on my own. 'You were not on your own', he said, 'and since you were planning a great "save the nursery campaign" I thought it was the moment to make clear that if you go on with this, and I hope you will, I cannot accompany you everywhere'. It was a sobering thought but not as chilling as I would have expected it to be. After all my friends in St Thomas' had experienced my fainting fits when I was a child; in fact Edna had been with me when I first fainted outside the home. I was quiet for a long time but after a while I knew I must not give up at this point and fetched pen and paper and wrote two furious letters, one to the *Oxford Mail* and the other to the *Oxford Times*. I repeated much of what I had said to the councillors about the background of the nurseries, putting great emphasis on the fact that a farthing only on the rate was all that was needed to preserve the educational and social benefits derived from the existence of all five nursery classes and making the point that many of the children attending the classes lacked any recreational facilities. I ended both letters by inviting parents and particularly those in the other four areas where their nursery class was about to be closed to join the St Thomas' parents in their fight. The response was overwhelming and a meeting was held in my house and the Parents' Committee

Our first home, 11 St Michael's Street

95 Iffley Road, to which we moved in 1953

Our tenant in both houses, Thomas Hugh Griffith (left), with Dr Percy

Holidays at Lee-on-Solent, with
the Lanchester and the family
(Simon on the left, Andrew on
the right)

formed. In addition to the parents the meeting was also attended to Bob Nimmo-Smith, the Chairman of the Oxford City Labour Party, and Thomas Hodgkin, the Secretary of the Oxford Extra Mural Delagacy, and also a University representative on the city's Education Committee who asked to attend as observers, and who gave us much-needed advice on how to proceed. We mounted a splendid campaign, speaking from snow-covered Co-op lorries in St Giles, collecting hundreds and hundreds of signatures for our petition and arranging a public meeting in the Assembly Room at the Town Hall where the chief speaker was Lady Simon of Wythenshaw. The meeting was packed and there was standing room only. St Thomas', old and young, was there in force, together with parents and grandparents from West Oxford, St Ebbes, South Oxford and New Hinksey. There were officers and members of the local National Union of Teachers, social workers, educationalists and other interested people including, again, Bob Nimmo-Smith and Thomas Hodgkin, this time accompanied by his wife, Dorothy.

Our campaign received the whole-hearted support of the National Union of Teachers and we got belated support from the city Labour Party due, no doubt, to the influence of Bob Nimmo-Smith, because the Labour councillors on the Education Committee had voted in favour of the closures. We also got excellent and sympathetic coverage from the *Oxford Mail* and *Oxford Times*. At one of the meetings in St Giles Edmund stood next to a man who turned to him and said, 'Doesn't that young woman speak well? Don't you think she would make a good councillor for the West Ward?'. 'No', replied Edmund, 'she is my wife and I don't know what it would do to her'.

The great day came. The City Council was to debate the recommendation of its Education Committee to close our nursery classes, and I sat in the public gallery which was filled to overflowing with angry and anxious parents. In spite of warnings we clapped when speakers supported us and muttered angrily when they didn't. The result, of course, was a compromise. An amendment was carried which closed three of the classes but kept open the other two, of which St Thomas' was one and South Oxford was the other. Far from being elated I was cast down. I had believed, in my political innocence, that if there was a case for two there was a case for all five. I ought to have been grateful for the fact that the debate was taking place only a few weeks before the local elections, otherwise we might not have gained anything at all. I was very upset that the councillors I had briefed had either not read my brief or had not understood it. I felt so sorry for the children and the parents of those nurseries which were going to close and I genuinely believed that if the right speeches had been made all five nurseries would have been saved. From this anger and frustration came the realisation that, however justified and vigorous a public protest is, change can only be achieved by organised politics. It was then only a small step for me to join the Labour Party for, believing as passionately as I do, in a socialist democracy, there could be no other political party for me. I have never, however, thought of it as 'this great party of mine' for a party is only as good as its members will allow it to be. I have loved and respected, and still do, many of my comrades within the Labour Party but I sometimes think its public image is far removed from the moral fervour of the Keir Hardie days when 'to each according to his needs and from each according to his means' was its guiding star.

I felt immediately at home in the West Ward branch of the Oxford Labour Party. They gave me a warm welcome and congratulated me on my nursery campaign which, surprisingly, they regarded as successful; obviously I had not then learned the art of compromise. Above all they were my kind of people and spoke the same language as I did. Surprisingly it contained no members from St Thomas, a loss I immediately set out to put right. In all I managed to persuade my father and about a dozen of my friends to become members but it was the devil's own job to get them to meetings as it is not, by nature, a clubbable community.

At my first meeting I was taken under the wing of Arthur Griffin, a retired railwayman and former councillor for the ward, who turned out to be the man who had expressed to Edmund in St Giles the view that I would make a good councillor for the West Ward. He was one of the best socialists I have ever known. His socialism was without personal bitterness and he believed passionately in the brotherhood of man and the emergence of a world at peace. He even shared my views on the Bomb which was unusual at that time. I shall always be grateful that he was my political mentor in those early days and helped me to develop my political philosophies within the confines of the party. He lost no time in attempting to get me to agree to stand for the Council. 'But Arthur', I said, 'I am not clever enough'. 'Clever', he replied with an amused grin, 'You should go and watch them in action'. 'I have', I said, 'at the nursery class debate, but I don't think that was a very good example because I don't think they knew very much about the subject'. 'I was there too', said Arthur, 'and to be honest it was one of their better efforts'. He then gave me some very sound advice on public speaking. 'Find out everything you can about the subject you are going to speak on. Never speak just for effect or say what your listeners want to hear if you don't believe it yourself'. In my ignorance it seemed such simple and obvious advice; yet over the years I have found such a high standard of personal integrity very difficult, and on occasions, impossible to achieve.

In May 1953 I became one of the West Ward Labour Party candidates for the local elections, convinced that I had, forever, put behind me all my ridiculous nervous problems.

The statutory requirements for becoming a councillor were, and still are, very few. One must be a British subject of twenty-one years, or over, and resident, or working within the boundaries of the Local Authority to which one is seeking election. One's candidature must be endorsed in writing by a proposer, a seconder, and ten supporters all of whom must be on the current electoral register of the particular ward. The disqualifications are not much of a deterrent either. You must not be an undischarged bankrupt, have spent more than three months in prison or be a certified lunatic. Disgruntled ratepayers have been heard to mutter, on occasions 'they may not be certified, but...'.

The reality of being selected and elected is far more difficult. In these days of the polarisation of politics the Independents has been virtually squeezed out of local government as they have been already lost to National Government. At the present moment Oxford City Council, with 45 members, has no Independent, and the Oxfordshire County Council with 70 members, has one. In the Labour Party, and I doubt if it is very different in other political parties, one goes through a rigorous set of procedures to become a candidate. First one has to be nominated for the election panel and this has to be endorsed, after seemingly endless and barbed questions by the local executive committee. Then on to a selection meeting, in the company of several other 'hopefuls', and if successful the final hurdle is the approval of the constituency Labour Party's general committee.

After this soul-searching exercise the job of canvassing the electorate seems comparatively easy and much less demoralising even if, at times, one has to face some unflattering truths. In all I fought fourteen elections in the West Ward (losing two) and thoroughly enjoyed each campaign. The Cox family had lived in St Thomas' for at least three hundred years for my ancestor Ralph Cox, a mat maker, is recorded as being admitted a Freeman of the City in 1664. A Council Minute of the 2 November 1663 states, 'Item att this Council it is agreed that Ralph Cox – Mattmaker shall be admitted into the Liberties of this Citie for the fyne of Twentie Nobles and the Officers' fees and a Bucket provided he give bond to pay £20 to this Citie when he useth any other Trade than a Mattmaker in the same'. He is also recorded in Salter's Oxford Acts as having paid window tax for a habitation in High Street St Thomas in 1667. His descendants, including my father, became hereditary freemen.

The West Ward is an interesting ward to represent, stretching from Walton Well Road in the north to the Oxford boundary at the western end of Botley Road, and including Port Meadow and the village of Binsey. When I was first elected it contained three predominantly working-class areas, St Thomas', Jericho and Osney Island, and these and many other parts of the ward housed the old Oxford families. Several colleges, many University lodging houses, offices and shops on the north side of Queen Street, the west side of Cornmarket Street and the whole of George Street, together with a sizeable distribution of industry, including the Oxford University Press and Lucy's Iron Works, are all in the ward. In those days it was largely conservative with a small as well as a large 'C'. Having lived in the ward all my life, for St Thomas', Botley Road and St Michael's Street were all within its boundaries, I was, of course, fairly well known and Edmund was fond of commenting that if all my cousins, my second cousins, and other relatives came out to vote, I was bound to get in with a large majority. This pre-supposed of course that they would vote for me for I was, after all, a prophet in my own country and most of them were very suspicious of people of our class who 'had ideas above their station'.

This familiarity with the electorate has its disadvantages as well as its advantages. Fellow canvassers often complained good naturedly that, in future, they were going to leave Olive at home when canvassing because she was forever disappearing, with the canvass cards, into houses and not reappearing until it was too late to continue. Heaven knows how many cups of tea, camp coffee and cocoa, and glasses of parsnip and rhubarb wine I have consumed on these occasions but I loved it all. No less entertaining were the comments to me, or other canvassers, on my ability and character.

Edmund was once canvassing in Jericho, not at that time a bastion of sex equality, and when he knocked on the door of a small terraced house it was opened by an elderly gentleman in braces and rolled up sleeves. 'I am canvassing on behalf of Olive Gibbs and Bill Fagg your two Labour candidates', Edmund began pleasantly. 'You're all right here', was the reply, 'I've been an active Trades Unionist all my life. I shall certainly vote for Mr Fagg'. 'Oh good', said Edmund 'and I hope you will be voting for Mrs Gibbs as well'. 'Certainly not', said the man, 'I wouldn't vote for her'. Edmund was a bit taken aback by his vehemence and asked him why he wouldn't vote for me as I was generally regarded as a good ward councillor. 'She's a woman', our good Trade Union friend replied, 'gadding about up at that Town Hall having the time of her life. And got a husband and two kids at home. The brazen hussy boasts about it in her election address. She ought to be ashamed of herself'. Edmund recognised defeat and was about to go when the chap pushed his finger into Edmund's chest and demanded, 'And what sort of man is her husband to allow her to do it? Gutless swine. I'd tell him a thing or two if ever I met him'. To his eternal shame Edmund assured this male chauvinist that he would pass on this message to Mr Gibbs when next he saw him. I was furious when I heard this story and demanded angrily of Edmund why he had not defended women's rights. 'No point in losing a vote for Bill Fagg as well', he said laconically.

On another occasion, however, he did react quite strongly to criticism of me. He was canvassing in one of the roads off Botley Road and was told by a woman that although she was a strong Labour supporter nothing would persuade her to vote for that ghastly Gibbs woman. 'What is wrong with her?', asked Edmund. 'Oh she is a terrible type', was the reply. 'The very worst kind of publicity-seeking exhibitionist'. 'Oh, come on', said my husband, 'she really isn't as bad as all that. I have been married to her for almost forty years'. 'Hard luck, mate', was the vehement response as the door was slammed in his face. He regarded the door thoughtfully for a bit and then gave it a good kick.

My views on unilateral nuclear disarmament, especially in the early years, have not always been acceptable to Labour Party supporters and in 1959 I had one of my frequent arguments on this subject, on the doorstep of a house in Duke Street. 'Oh no, Mrs Gibbs', the man said, 'I can't vote for you because I don't like your views on the Hydrogen Bomb'. I told him I was sorry about this but I couldn't change my views in order to get a vote and then went on to ask him why he thought Britain should keep the Bomb. 'We got to keep it', he told me, 'to keep us safe'. 'Against whom?', I innocently enquired. 'Against the Americans' was his immediate reply. For a few seconds I was at a loss for speech and he took the opportunity of telling me confidentially and apologetically that he was a good Labour supporter normally and had voted for my son two years before. 'My son?', I exclaimed, 'Yes', he said, 'Councillor Edmund Gibbs'. 'That's not my son, that's my husband', I explained. 'Cor Missus you do surprise me', he reacted. I exploded and proceeded to tell him that if he were so bloody stupid as to believe we were spending millions of pounds defending ourselves from our allies and that my husband was my son, then the Tories were welcome to his vote. I didn't want it. I wonder what a psephologist would make of the fact that he has had a Tory poster in his window ever since!

At that time of my first election the West Ward had six councillors representing it (two being eligible for election each year and thereafter serving a three year term of office) but in 1953 when I stood there were three vacancies as a previous councillor had resigned after two years. Except for Edgar Smewin, who lived in St Barnabas and was now an Alderman, the West Ward, with isolated exceptions, elected Conservative councillors, but in 1952, due no doubt to the nursery campaign, two Labour candidates, Beesley and Kynnersley, were returned to the City Council. This put new heart into the West Ward Labour Party and we fought a vigorous campaign, much helped by Edmund's flair for organisation, although he had not yet joined the party. My reputation from the nursery campaign and my family's long connections with the ward stood me in good stead but the fact that I was a woman did not. At my selection meeting doubts had been expressed and two or three votes cast against me, in the belief that a woman could not win the West Ward. My strongest supporter was Mrs Ivy Jones, J.P., the chairman of the ward party, who had done magnificent work in the ward but had stood unsuccessfully in six elections. This was a great comfort to me because, sadly, most of the antipathy came from women themselves and it is significant that the only woman to be elected for the West Ward before me was Miss Hughes in 1908, almost fifty years earlier and before women had the vote.

The West Ward Tories were, I think, surprised at the thoroughness of our canvass for we called at every house in the ward, something which had never before been attempted. We also had a great many helpers both from inside and outside the party. The Tories themselves, having received an unexpected defeat the year before, were well prepared though and on election day itself the streets in the ward were filled with cars plastered with blue posters. By tea-time it was obvious to me that we had lost the election for our returns showed that only one out of every three votes had been cast for us. What I did not know, but what the 'old hands' repeatedly assured me of, was that Labour traditionally voted in the evening when the men, having returned from work and had a meal, took their wives to the poll. When the polling booths closed at 9 pm Edmund was fairly sure that it would be a very close vote with the Tories just having the edge over us.

We retired to the Fire Station in George Street where the votes were to be counted just after 9 pm. I had never been to a 'count' before; a policeman checked our names on a list as we went in and then there was a nail-biting period when ballot papers were emptied from their tin boxes on to various trestle tables and counted by staff, employed by the Town Hall, to check that the numbers corresponded with the total number of voting papers recorded as having been handed in at each polling station. The proceedings were presided over by the Returning Officer who in those days was an Alderman, with no previous political connections with the ward, and who was therefore deemed to be impartial. On this occasion, and for many years afterwards, our Returning Officer was Alderman Mrs Harrison-Hall, a retired General Practitioner who had been a Conservative councillor for the East Ward. She had also been a member of the Library Committee when I worked in the City Library and a close friend of Peggy Campbell. She greeted me with a warm smile which put me at my ease in these somewhat awe-inspiring surroundings, but considerably annoyed some of the Tories there. (Three years ago, at the opening of the new Law Courts in Oxford, her son Judge Michael Harrison-Hall introduced himself to me and told me his mother was always very fond of me). The voting was as close as Edmund had expected it to be and it was impossible to foretell the result until it was actually announced.

Duke	(Conservative)	1564 votes	Elected for 3 years
Mrs Gibbs	(Labour)	1526 votes	Elected for 3 years
Gillett	(Conservative)	1470 votes	Elected for One year

Dossett	(Labour)	1462 votes Not elected
Walton	(Labour)	1337 votes Not elected
Mrs Bryan-Brown	(Conservative)	1331 votes Not elected

A great cheer went up from the members of the West ward Labour Party who were delighted we now had three of the six Council seats in the Ward but again, as with the nursery class vote, my feelings were mixed. I found it difficult to believe that I had actually been elected a councillor for the next three years and I was desperately sorry for Dick Dossett who had been an excellent 'running partner' and had lost by only eight votes. I felt we had not done enough to muster those extra votes and when I learned afterwards that we ought to have demanded a 'recount' I felt even worse. Dick was plainly disappointed but he was generous in his praise of me and we have been friends ever since.

When we came out of the Fire Station, half of St Thomas', including my Dad, were waiting outside in Gloucester Green to congratulate me and, chattering and laughing, most of them came home with us to celebrate. Mr Griffith was waiting at the door of St Michael's Street to hear the result and he actually overcame his dislike of 'ugly faces' to join us in a drink. He solemnly told the assembled company that he had forsaken the Conservative cause for the first time, to vote for me, but added that 'none of us should forget that it was Winston Churchill who had won the war'.

My last waking thought that night was 'At least you have struck a blow for St Thomas' and for women'.

When I became a councillor I had been a member of the Labour Party for just over a year and during that period the realisation slowly dawned on me that, in some quarters and not least in the hierarchy of the Labour Group, I was regarded as a dangerous left-winger. I was shocked and bewildered by this. Edmund had warned me before I joined the Labour Party that, although I then had few, if any enemies, once I became involved in party politics I might find it difficult to know where my friends were. I scornfully dismissed this jaundiced view putting it down to a cynicism about politics in general which he had inherited from his father. It was obvious that my views on the Bomb and my passionate belief in the social and educational values of comprehensive education were not then in line with the mainstream thinking of the Labour Party. But it was not just this that worried them; the distrust of me had far deeper roots.

The shadow of the Patrick Gordon Walker episode still hung over the party; my father-in-laws' pronounced left wing views and my participation in left wing demonstrations before the war had aroused their suspicions. These were then confirmed by the fact that the Parents' Committee, of which I was the secretary had, as its Chairman, Mick Leahy who was a communist. They paid no heed to the fact that Mick had a child in the West Oxford nursery class nor that the Treasurer was a Conservative and the majority of the committee had no political allegiances at all. It was again a case of 'guilt by association'. Having been so used to the left wing coalition of the late thirties, and holding the naïve view that the last war had been fought, and so many of our years laid waste by it, in the cause of freedom I was horrified. This attitude confirmed all my previous fears of the restrictions of party politics and how fundamentally unsuited I was for a party machine. But I do not give in easily to pressures and, uncomfortable though I found it all, I thought they would have to throw me out before I got out.

Not long after my election and before I went to my first Council meeting the Leader of the Labour Group, Marcus Lower, called to see me at my home, gave me a long, boring and sanctimonious speech on what was expected of me and then, patting me paternally on the shoulder, delivered his pièce de résistance. 'Once you have got rid of these silly ideals of yours you will make a very good councillor, Olive'. I think even he was surprised at the vehemence of my reply. 'I hope I am dead before I lose my ideals and if the Labour Party had not lost so many of theirs they might have won the 1951 election'.

After this exchange it was not altogether surprising that when I took my seat in the Council Chamber, the Labour Group, numbering eighteen and including two other women, Kathleen Lower, Headington and Doris Rees from Cowley, did not show me any marked enthusiasm, although Beesley and Kynnersley, for whom I had worked so hard the year before, gave me a guarded welcome. Edgar Smewin was friendly enough but he was rather a remote character; I had never seen him at a West Ward Labour Party meeting and I understood he rarely attended Group meetings. It was left to Alderman Mrs Andrews a Conservative, who had known Edmund's father when they were both representing the South Ward, to say how pleased she was to see another woman on the Council and especially a younger one. Moreover she showed me where the Members' Common Room was and, of paramount importance, the Ladies' Cloakroom. The lack of warmth shown me by the Labour Group was not shared by the Town Clerk, Harry Plowman, and other Council officers. In my view, and the view of many others, Harry Plowman was one of the finest Town Clerks local government has ever known. He was an astute lawyer, steeped in the traditions of good local government, absolutely fair and easily accessible to any member of the Council, or his staff, from the Mayor to the office boy. He must have held political views, but they were never obvious and he had that great virtue, often so lacking in local government, of a sense of humour accompanied by laughter. When he died in office in 1965 I was desolated not only by a sense of personal loss at his death but at the passing of an era. I was surprised, too, to find that many of the senior officers of the Council had been fellow members of NALGO with me; I had even known some of them from school-days and the mutual trust we established was a great strength throughout my years as a councillor.

I sat in the seat, well below the salt, allocated to me and, except for an occasional trip to the Sheriff's or Lord Mayor's chairs, never changed it during my time on the City Council even when I became Leader of the Labour Group and, eventually, the 'Mother of Council'. I hoped it would serve to remind me, when I needed reminding, that all men (and women) are born equal and that 'rank' is an artificial, if convenient, distinction. I often wonder whether the present occupier has ever been able to erase the indelibly inked message 'To the Barricades, Sister' written in the drawer of the attached desk by some unknown admirer or critic.

There were sixty-eight members of the Oxford City Council which was then a County Borough; forty-two were elected councillors from the seven wards of the City: West, South, North, East, Summertown and Wolvercote, Headington and Marston, Cowley and Iffley. In addition there were nine councillors from the University: six elected by Heads and Bursars of Colleges and three by Convocation. For each three councillors there was one Alderman, the Council itself electing those from the wards and the University representatives electing their own. The Aldermen all served for a six year period of office but they were eligible for re-election and tended to be a self-perpetuating body. One of the few advantages arising from the reorganisation of local government in 1974 was the abolition of University representation, the Aldermanic Bench and other forms of undemocratic government. (In 1967 the Privy Council, on a 'prayer' from the City Council, had already reduced the number of University representatives from twelve to eight; six councillors, all to be elected from Congregation, and two Aldermen).

In those early years the Conservatives, ably led by their formidable Leader, Lady Townsend, were in overwhelming control of the Council and yet many of their major committees, such as Education, Watch (Police) and Estates, were chaired by University members.

At my first meeting I gazed nervously around and, in spite of Arthur Griffin's reassurance as to my ability, I felt woefully inadequate wondering if I would ever be able to cope with committee reports, amendments, motions and all the other complicated issues of local government; not least its standing orders. At some point during that meeting, when I was feeling at my most desperate, I pulled myself together and discovered a personal philosophy which has been of immeasurable help to me during the whole of my public and political life. 'Gibbs, you are average and that means, in any given situation, forty-nine and a half per cent of the people in the room are more intelligent than you are, but forty-nine and a half per cent are a damned sight more stupid'. There are obvious flaws in this philosophy but it has been a great comfort to me over the years and I still recommend it to the nervous.

My other first impression of that gathering of the City fathers was that it was overwhelmingly male and mostly agèd. With a few women there it resembled nothing so much as 'Ladies' night' at an Old Boys' club. A great many of them looked older than God, and not safe out after dark, and I vowed to myself there and then that if local government did not impose an age limit on its members I would set my own and if I were still there at sixty-five I would resign. I was and I did, for I was not prepared to listen to the arguments urged on me that 'age is comparative'. The tragedy as I see it is that when senility approaches it is never recognised by oneself and even if other people are too kind to mention it one would not believe it if they did. But there were thirty glorious, battle-filled years before that day arrived.

13 · HOME

As well as becoming a councillor, I saw other major changes in 1953 and at the end of that year we moved from St Michael's Street to our present house on the Iffley Road and for the first time in our thirteen years of married life we had a home we could really call our own.

I never liked living in St Michael's Street for, apart from the gloomy atmosphere of it, I lived constantly in a state of tension for my mother-in-law, who still officially held the lease, was critical of the few minor alterations we made, and never failed to let us know that it was her house and she would return there sooner or later. At the beginning of the summer of that year Percy Christian, her husband, had a heart attack, and I felt that as far as my mother-in-law's return was concerned it was going to be sooner rather than later. I knew that sharing a house with her, for any length of time, would not be possible for me and moreover I suspected that it would not be so much 'sharing' as living as her lodgers. I talked my fears over with Edmund and he saw the problem but wondered where, with the limited amount of capital we had, we could find a house which would accommodate the two of us, Andrew, Simon and Midge, and, of immediate concern to me, Mr Griffith. I knew I could not leave him behind because he was, by now, so much part of our family, and I knew he did not want to live with my mother-in-law again. Poor Thomas Hugh; when I mentioned our difficulties to him he said at once that he would go into a nursing home in Weybridge where he had friends but I would not hear of it, even if the annuity he had bought over thirty years before would meet the cost, and his relief was touchingly obvious.

Shortly after my talk with Edmund I went across the road to the auctioners and estate agents Mallam, Payne, and Dorn and asked to see Mr Weeks who was one of the partners there with whom I was quite friendly. I explained our dilemma to him and asked whether he had any 'properties' on his books which would meet our rather specialised needs, little capital and an extended family. He gave me a cup of coffee, listened sympathetically and commented that it was a 'tall order' and that here was no such house on his books at the moment. He went on to say that he would let me know immediately should he hear of any such property. The weeks dragged past; Percy's health slowly deteriorated, much to my sorrow for I was very fond of him, and I wondered what on earth our future was to be.

Towards the middle of August, while we were at Lee, I received a letter from Mr Weeks saying he thought he had found a house on the Iffley Road which would suit us and it was being put up for public auction in the first week in September. He very much hoped we would be back in time for it. I was all for returning to Oxford there and then but as Edmund pointed out, if we returned at the end of August, as we had planned, we should not only be in time for the auction but would have an opportunity to look around the house beforehand. We arrived home on the Sunday evening and I waited in a fever of impatience for Mr Weeks' office to open at 9 am. He had scarcely put his key in the lock before I darted across the road to bombard him with questions. 'Was it big enough for us?' 'Could I have the keys to go and see it?' 'Was it empty?' The answer to all these questions was 'Yes', and he invited me into his office to give me further details. It was an old house, built in 1870, which was originally a farmhouse attached to a small-holding stretching through to the Cowley Road. The area around it was now built-up but it was at the end of a terrace with a drive-way at the side. It had nine rooms, in addition to a bathroom and kitchen, plus an 'outside' lavatory. It also had a splendid view across the Iffley Road Running Ground (where we later watched Roger Bannister run the first four minute mile) over to the Berkshire Hills. It appeared to be a dream house but Mr Weeks was quick to explain that following the death of the previous owner it had been empty for several months, and was in a very bad state of repair.

I rushed back home with the keys tightly grasped in my hand and described the house to Edmund who said that we would go and view it that evening. 'This evening?', I said, 'I can't wait that long; I am going up there now'. From the moment I first saw it, I loved that house; it had a kind of quaint crooked look about it. Although three-storeyed it appeared dwarfed by the adjoining houses and, while their roofs were grey-slated, mine, for I already regarded it as such, had warm red tiles. I was enchanted by the curious unsymmetrical aspect of its front windows, for the bottom one was out of alignment with those on the first and second floors and it was this which gave the house its crooked appearance.

My excitement was such that I could hardly turn the key in the lock, but a quick look round soon confirmed Mr Weeks' warning that it was not in a state of good repair, although his statement that it had been empty for several months was not quite accurate, for it was perfectly obvious that it had been occupied by a tramp for a considerable part of that period. There were large damp patches on most of the walls but the paper hanging from them was no loss for it was quite the most hideous wall-paper I have ever seen; the paintwork too was dark brown, reminding me, depressingly, of my childhood. The kitchen had an uneven brick floor with an enormous stone-built copper in the corner. The garden was a small, insect-infested, jungle. But nothing quenched my enthusiasm. I loved it and it just had to be my home.

Edmund, when he viewed it that evening, was less enthusiastic but conceded that, with repairs and redecoration, 'it would do for the time being'. We returned the keys to Mr Weeks the next morning and, when we told him we were interested in the house and intended being at the auction on Thursday, he advised us, rather more kindly than

Lord Mayor of Oxford 1982

Celebration of the 25th anniversary of the founding of CND, 17 February 1983. From left to right: Michael Foot, Bruce Kent, Pat Arrowsmith, Annajoy David, O.G., Joan Ruddock, Sir Richard Acland. *Photograph, Press Association*

Chairman of the County Council. The opening of the Faringdon bypass by Lynda Chalker, Minister of State for Transport, 1985. *Photograph, Oxford and County Newspapers*

professionally I suspect, to start the bidding at £1,600 but not to go above £1,950 as it needed so much doing to it. Tuesday and Wednesday dragged painfully past and we arrived fifteen minutes early at the auction which was in a large room at the back of Mallam, Payne and Dorn's offices. I was amazed to see so many people already there. The room was packed and Mr Weeks hurried across to us, with a worried expression on his face, and whispered that he had not expected the sale of the house to arouse so much interest, but to remember the advice he had given us.

I had never been to an auction before (nor since!) and I was shaken at the speed with which the bids were made. Edmund, with true accountant's caution, firmly began the bidding with an offer of £1,550 but in no time at all, with a nod here, a wink there and the surreptitious lift of a paper from various corners of the room, the price quickly rose by fifty pound bids to £1,850. At this point, with possible defeat staring us in the face, Edmund bid £1875 but with clockwork regularity the offers soon reached £1950. People now began to drift away and, in desperation, I begged Edmund to go as far as £2000, to which he reluctantly agreed. That point being reached and passed, he announced that he was going home and advised me to do the same. When, with a lump in my throat, I refused saying I wanted to see how much the house finally fetched, he left me with a final injunction not to bid so much as an extra penny for it. After £2,250 the bidding slowed down to ten pound bids and at £2340 the offers appeared to have finished. Mr Weeks raised his hammer and said, like some religious incantation, 'I am bid £2340, £2340, are there any further advances on £2340?'. Silence ensued and when he raised his hammer for the final blow, it was more than I could bear. In a loud, clear, firm voice which I hoped would indicate that I was prepared to go on forever I offered £2350. There was a hush, followed by the sound of indrawn breaths, and my dear friend, Mr Weeks, with an anxious look on his face, gabbled £2350, £2350, and brought down the hammer with excessive speed announcing that the property, 95 Iffley Road, had been acquired by Mrs Gibbs. I was terrified at what I had done; I could not give Mr Weeks a cheque, as I did not even possess a cheque book in those days, but I told him that Edmund would come over later and pay him.

I crept home and Edmund came out of the sitting room and enquired how much it had fetched. 'Two thousand, three hundred ad fifty pounds', I said. 'Good Lord', commented my husband, 'What fool bought it at that price?'. 'I did', I replied and burst into tears. Faced with this 'fait accompli' Edmund groaned and said, 'Oh, my God, where are we going to find the money?' I was now even more frightened as I did not know whether I might not have been guilty of some criminal act and be on a charge of false pretences, but Edmund, of course, did find the money.

One of his nicest clients lent him a sum which covered the discrepancy between our bank balance and the price of the house. Another client, Eddie Smith a builder, gave him an estimate for essential repairs and armed with this Edmund approached a Building Society which lent him all the money he needed to cover the cost of the house and the repairs. I don't know who was most relieved by this happy ending, my dear Mr Weeks, or me! Ten days after that fateful auction Percy Christian died, and my mother-in-law announced her intention of moving back into St Michael's Street in time for Christmas. Eddie Smith and his workmen laboured unremittingly to finish the work, and on 15 December, the day after Edmund's thirty-fifth birthday, we moved into '95'. Edmund, Midge and the two boys came up here in the furniture van and I followed in a taxi with Mr Griffith and the cat. I don't know which was the more apprehensive of the two, Thomas Hugh or the cat, but it was the cat which made the most strenuous efforts to escape.

Two of our 'lodgers', David Grant-Adamson and Andrew Macintosh, joined us in the evening. Although they had originally intended to find other 'digs', more centrally situated, they both came to the conclusion that the mile to Carfax was a small price to pay for remaining with us.

14 · NOT THE END

I cannot pinpoint exactly when it was I first realised that the 'psychological hang-ups' I thought I had banished forever were slowly beginning to return but it was before we changed houses because I remember the anguish with which I received the news that the Post Office, because of a long waiting list, could not install a telephone at '95' for months, maybe a year. On Christmas Day, ten days after we moved, Simon developed Scarlet Fever and, although my GP, Dr Sweet, assured me that it was not now the dangerous disease it had been in my youth, as its virulence had disappeared, and that Simon would not have to go to hospital, I was desperately worried. Haunted by memories of Andrew's illnesses I wondered what on earth I would do if Simon became worse and I could not telephone the doctor immediately. Simon, of course, quickly recovered but there was no such recovery for me and the New Year brought increasing problems.

I missed many Council meetings and, eventually, Council itself and with each absence my conscience troubled me more and more as I felt I was letting the West Ward and its people down. After a bit I could bear it no longer and told Edmund that I intended resigning my seat. He was horrified for I think he felt that my interest in Council work could prove my salvation and he advised me to do two things: firstly to see my doctor and take him into my confidence; secondly to write to Harry Plowman informing him, as Town Clerk, that for personal and domestic reasons I could not attend any meetings of Council for two or three months; an absence of longer than six months would need the permission of Council itself. To please Edmund because he had been so patient with me over so many years I followed his advice but I did not believe that there was any cure for my kind of illness and was convinced that I would live the rest of my life in a state of semi-paralysis. Dr Sweet was much more cheerful. 'You are doing far too much', he said, 'Cosset yourself a bit; buy some new clothes, have a different hairstyle; change the furniture around'. When I suggested to him that perhaps I ought to see a psychiatrist, he was adamantly opposed to it. 'What good will that do you?', he asked, 'Your mind is healthy enough'. I have nothing but affection, respect and gratitude for Bert Sweet, for he was a marvellous family doctor and, later, friend to us; his kindness and attention to us all was over and above his professional obligation but, like many members of his profession some thirty years ago, he had his doubts about the value of psychiatry. To calm and help me to sleep he gave me a bottle of chalk-like medicine which I afterwards discovered was a much watered down mixture of phenobarbitone.

I rarely left the shelter of my home, until one day, in the middle of February, when I was telephoned by Michael Foot (M.R.D. Foot, a cousin of the famous Michael) who was a member of the Labour Party; a history don at New College, and who had been chosen to fight a Council by-election in South Ward. He wanted to know whether I would help him in his election as I knew so many people in the South Ward and understood, better than most, the problems of the older areas of the city. My first reaction was to say 'No' but I could not bring myself to disappoint him without offering some kind of explanation and I asked him to come and see me. He came that evening and was the first person, other than Dr Sweet and my family, to learn of my problems. He was very upset, much more for me than for the loss of my canvassing, and begged me to let him know if there were any way in which he could help. I felt dreadful after he had gone and the next day I gathered together any remnants of strength I had left and telephoned him saying that if he or his wife would collect me I would make an effort to canvass. It says much for Michael that he immediately agreed for he was justified in believing that in my mental state I would be much more of a hindrance than a help in his election. Curiously enough this did not prove to be the case because, as with the Nursery Campaign, I threw everything I had into that election, canvassing every day except at weekends and speaking at all his political meetings. He won, with a creditable majority, and I went entirely to pieces.

Life was a nightmare for everyone living at 95 Iffley Road. I screamed every time Edmund left the house; I could not eat and I could not sleep and I could not bear to let the children out of my sight although I am sure those were the only happy periods they had. My family had to put up with it, but why Midge, David and Andrew did I cannot explain, for it lasted several weeks. It all culminated in a medical depression. I had always thought that a depression was just feeling a bit low, until I experienced one which lasted for about two hours. It is a physical as well as a mental assault on the body. I could take neither food nor drink; the food just lodged half-way down my throat and I thought I would choke. I could not speak and nothing or no-one could make any impression on me. I was wrapped in a shroud of impenetrable and absolute sadness and I curled up on my bed and prayed to die. Edmund phoned Dr Sweet who came at once and was in time to witness the last half an hour of that awful depression. In spite of his previously-held view, that there was nothing much wrong with me which a change wouldn't cure, he rang the Park Hospital at Headington and made an appointment for me to attend a clinic there the following afternoon.

I was never quite clear what the difference between the Warneford Hospital and the Park Hospital was. They were both National Health Hospitals for patients with psychiatric problems; located on the same site but some way apart, administered by the same Management Committee and served mainly by the same medical team. The Park stressed that it was a hospital for nervous functional disorders so whether this meant that we, in the Park, were expected to be short-term patients while the Warneford catered for longer term patients I don't know but I have always suspected that the distinction was social.

My appointment to see a Dr Davidson was for 3 pm but although we arrived early we did not get into see him until 3.30 pm. The tension of waiting in that prefabricated hut which served as his consulting rooms stretched my nerves to such an extent that I thought they would snap like over-extended elastic and I begged Edmund to take me home which, sensibly, he refused to do. My first impression of Sam Davidson was one of a mild shock, and then resentment. He was fairly short with thick black hair, 'pebble' glasses, and a very soft voice. But what really worried me was that he looked so young; I learned later that he was twenty-seven years old. I already had my doubts about the value of psychiatrists as I believed that, while they could delve into my past and tell me why I had the problems I had, since it was impossible to erase the past they surely could not cure me. His youth was the last straw, for what possible experience of life could this young man have that would, in any way, help him to understand mine? Having read my doctor's report he asked me several questions to which I gave short irritable answers, revealing as little as I could. I am sure he was no more impressed by me than I was by him, but after talking to Edmund a bit he suggested that I came into the Park Hospital for a month. I was aghast at the suggestion feeling that incarceration, as I regarded it, in a hospital away from Edmund and the family would be all that was need-ed to unhinge me completely. I rudely refused his offer saying that I had expected to be treated as an out-patient not as the inmate of a men-tal institution. Sam's patience must have been wearing very thin but he said quietly that he was sorry I would not take his advice, and of course he would see me as an out-patient but, quite frankly, he did not believe I would benefit from it as what I needed at that moment was sustained care.

We came home, Edmund very white, but not offering a word of reproach for my abominable behaviour, and that evening I had my second depression which again lasted for two hours. When I came out of it I knew I must never again impose this strain on Edmund and the boys. I asked Edmund to order me a taxi, while I packed my bag, and to take me to the Park Hospital and ask them to admit me as a patient. I did not deserve such consideration but they admitted me without demur or reproach when I arrived at 10 pm and shortly afterwards Sam Davidson came in, gave me a large sleeping pill and an even larger smile, and simply said, 'I am glad you changed your mind, Mrs Gibbs'.

I do not know enough about psychiatry to explain the details of my treatment or explain how Sam cured me by teaching me how to cope with life, but he did. I was in such a bad state when I arrived that he, and the Director of the Park Hospital, Dr Berkenau, discussed giving me 'shock' treatment but decided to wait and see how I responded to other treatment before seeking my permission for such extreme action. As it turned out it wasn't necessary; for the first week I was fairly heavily drugged and slept for much of the time. After that I was subjected to twice daily sessions with Dr Davidson. He questioned me so closely about so many aspects of my life and at times his questions were so personal that I became very angry and told him what I thought about psychiatry in general, and him in particular, which wasn't very flattering. The angrier I got the more satisfied he appeared to be and one day after a particularly gruelling session I sought an interview with Dr Berkenau and asked if I could change my psychiatrist. 'You can if you like, Mrs Gibbs', he said with his gentle smile, 'but it would be a great pity if you did because Dr Davidson feels your views on life coincide very closely with his and he is very anxious you should be cured so that you can continue with your various activities'. He added, 'Don't get too upset when you fly in a temper because it is good for you to release your feelings in this way and, moreover, Dr Davidson learns far more about you during your outbursts of fury than he does when you are more contained'!

Sam Davidson taught me a great deal about myself, some of which I already knew and much that I did not. He underlined my strengths and emphasised my weaknesses. Far from being the self-assured person other people thought I was, I was in constant need of reassurance because my father had instilled in me, at an early age, a lack of confidence. My fainting fits were not 'medical' but a subconscious desire to escape from unbearable situations, especially violence. He could do nothing to help except to assure me that I should not be ashamed of them or regard them as a weakness. Nor could he do anything about my 'anxiety neurosis' except to explain, what I probably already knew, that 99 per cent of the things I worried about would never happen but that, in itself, would not stop me from worrying. Because of these strains I must, from time to time, stop, take stock of a situation and, if necessary, retreat. 'What on earth do you mean by that?', I asked, 'You must summon the strength to run away from battles you cannot win', he replied. 'But won't that mean I shall be running away from everything in life which proves difficult?'. 'No', he said, 'because you will be surprised, and perhaps upset, to learn that you have inherited all your father's aggressive tendencies. But aggression is not in itself a vice', he continued, 'it can be a valuable weapon in the fight for the more just society you so obviously want to see'.

I left the Park Hospital after three weeks there and returned to see Sam as an outpatient. I was surprised when in 1955 he wrote to me, between visits, asking me to go and see him and I wondered what it was about. I was stunned when he told me that he, and his family, were going to live in Israel, for only then did I realise how dependent I still was on him, that always in the back of my mind was the thought that he was there in the background and I could always call on him if necessary. With tears streaming down my face I said all this and told him that I did not think I could survive without him. 'I am confident that that will not happen', he said, 'But if you have so little confidence in yourself that you allow it to happen then you will not only have failed yourself you will have failed me'. I never again returned to the Park. After he had gone we corresponded at fairly regular intervals but only met twice, the last time in 1984, thirty years after I first became his patient and two years before his untimely death, from a heart attack, in 1986. It was typical of that great, but simple man, who had had such a distinguished career and won an international reputation in psychiatry that he should have been so delighted that my life had followed the pattern he had anticipated and he was unashamedly pleased with my modest achievements and the campaigns I had been involved in.

He was, I think, disappointed that I had never sought to be a Member of Parliament and had turned down several offers of nomination for a parliamentary seat, including Oxford. Yet he understood better than most my need for the warmth and security of family life. Edmund once laughingly commented that 'the poor girl has a pair of shoes which automatically march towards a banner whether she is wearing the damned things or not' but this flippancy glosses over his influence on my life which has been immeasurable. My weaknesses are my own but my strengths have come from his loving support, loyalty, and constant reassurance. I admire, respect, and am grateful to those women, in the House of Commons, who have faced the challenge but I have never regretted my choice and would not exchange my lot for that of anyone else.

Edmund was wrong when, on seeing 95 Iffley Road for the first time, he said that 'it would do for the time being': thirty-five years later we are still here. Although the character of the Iffley Road has changed so much in the last thirty years, family houses disappearing and being replaced by student hostels and other institutional uses, at least this house has retained its family use much to the pleasure of City planners. It is true that fifteen or so years ago I complained that the house was too big for me to cope with but when Edmund suggested we should look for a smaller house I was horrified. 'Move from here?', I exclaimed, 'I am never going to move from here'. Edmund's reply really shocked me. 'Well', he said calmly, 'I don't know how we shall get the coffin down those winding stairs'. 'The coffin can either go out as the wardrobe came in, through the window', I snapped, 'or I will take great care to die downstairs'. 'Oh that's a good idea', he said, 'Let's convert it and include in the plans a two-bedroomed downstairs flat'.

And so it came about that we again have an extended family dwelling. Andrew, Carol and their two children, Mark and Ellen, living in the three-bedroomed maisonette and we in the flat, with an invasion from the 'Headington Assyrians', Simon and Caroline with Melanie, Geoffrey and Becky, at weekends. Sadly there are not the children on the Iffley Road for my grandchildren to play with as there were for my two sons at the same age, and Edmund remarks wistfully that the Cricketers' Arms is no longer the 'local' it once was but a drinking centre for students. But one can't have everything and we have most things.

INDEX

INDEX